Broads on the Boards:

Strong roles for strong women actors

Kathy Coudle-King

Purchase of this collection does not afford production rights. Please contact the author at katking@dakotalit.com for permission to perform work in part or its entirety, as per the Dramatist Guild of America's guidelines.

Photo courtesy of Kenny Gray, Kenny Gray Photography: http://kennygray.com/kenny-2/

To Kelly, my warrior woman.

CONTENTS

Kathleen Coudle-King

Contents (continued)

Kathleen Coudle-King

Contents (continued)

18. Scary Tales (10+)   59

19. Cookies (10+)   62

20. Catching Fish (from Trees, 40+)   64

Ten-Minute Plays & One Acts

21. Mourning Coffee (65+)   68

22. Couple of Boobs (40 & 20+)   75

23. Someone Borrowed, Someone Blue (20s)   82

24. The Hole Story (50s)   94

25. Leonora, the Dancing Queen (50+)   106

25. The Calabozo (20+)   111

26. Las Soldaderas (17+)   117

27. Club Sandwich (40s/60s)   129

28. Women with Wrinkles (30/70s)   141

Production History   201

4

ACKNOWLEDGMENTS

The collection you hold in your hand represents more than two decades of work, so there are many people to acknowledge and many people I am sure I will miss due to a poor memory not an ungrateful heart.

First off, I want to thank my partner in life, Alan King, whose support for 25-plus years has never wavered. He took my writing seriously when I had my own misgivings. It was his support that allowed me to retreat to Starry Night in Truth or Consequences, NM to compile this collection. It was the financial support of the Dept. of English and the University of ND that made the retreat possible. And it was the generosity of the ND Museum of Art, Laurel Reuter and Matt Wallace, who provided me with a quiet place on the prairie to edit the final proof.

Pressing rewind, it was the UND Women's Center, Nancy Nienhuis and Kay Mendick, who in 1992 offered me the role of playwright-in-residence. This assignment and the plays I wrote (*Flesh & Bones, Women with Wrinkles,* and *Betty Crocker*) during my two years there helped me find my voice as a playwright. Women's stories. They so fascinated me, emboldened and inspired me, yet I didn't see them being represented on the American stage. Since that time, my focus has generally been on telling the stories of contemporary and historical women.

I've been fortunate to have had my work affirmed by friends who became directors, and directors who became friends, namely Adonica Schultz Aune, John Thompson, Becky Becker, and Sarah Thames, as well as others who have directed my short plays, and/or selected them for publication. I have the Dayton FutureFest to thank for pushing *Trees,* along, the Larry Corse International New Play Award, Association of Theatre in Higher Education (Denver), and the Hotchkiss school for believing in Compañeras, and Devanand Janki at NYU's Stella Adler Lab for seeking out *St. Bette's* and providing its premiere, and NJ Rep for "Someone Borrowed, Someone Blue." While "Kathy Coudle-King" will never be a household name in theatre circles, all of these people and audiences have en-*couraged* me to keep telling these stories. Without that courage, I would have stopped a long, long time ago. I thank you all.

And to Ryan, Kelly, Casey, and Sean -- I continue to watch with delight as your stories unfold.

1 "DRIPPINGS"

a monologue
for the victims of Hurricane Katrina
*GLADYS is a woman in her 70s, dressed in a housecoat and slippers.
There's a kitchen table, s.l., with two bottles of water on it. There's a
chair next to the table. GLADYS enters.*

GLADYS
Here, Baby!
(whistles)
You seen my dog? She's a big one. Her mama was a
bloodhound, her daddy a Shepherd. She looks like a monster
but she's just a big baby. Oh, where'd she get herself to? I
opened the door a bit ago to see if the water's gone down any -
- it hadn't -- I sure hope she didn't get out on me. Turned my
back for just an -- .
(She opens door and stares out)
I would've seen her.
(Closes door)
She's in here somewhere. Maybe hiding under the table.
Taking a nap. That where you at, Baby? Under the table?
(She leans down but gets dizzy.)
Whoa! Better just have a seat for a second.

Lord, it's hot! Look at me – the water's just pouring off. Been
pouring off for days. I just can't seem to - get dry. Look at
this –*(rings out the hem of her dress)*

GLADYS (CONT.)

Water. Water. Everywhere. Squeezing outta my pores. My hair, my clothes, this house, this city, this state, the whole damn coast! Is there a dry place left in this country? Cause if there is, point me to it. Just turn me in the right direction, and me and Baby be on our way. Baby?
(Sits and listens)
Must be sleepin'. Let sleeping dogs lie, they say. Dogs and babies. Dogs and babies.

You know what I learned in this whole mess? Aside from the fact the government isn't worth a fart -- I learned that most folks take "dry" for granted. You do, dontcha? You wet you just assume you'll get dry -- eventually. You take a shower, you get a nice, fluffy towel, you pat yourself off, rub yourself dry. You go for a swim in a lake. You get out, sit in the sun, and you dry off in no time. Me? I can't assume that no more. No way, honey. Can't do that here. Ain't a dry towel to be had. Now everything's sticky and wet. Sticky and wet. Smells like chicken done gone foul – ha! -- and something -- worse. Water all around here, making my little house an island. Always wanted to visit one of them islands – the Bahamas, Bermuda, something like that. But this? Careful what you pray for, honey, cause the Lord? He's an old man with bad hearing. And lately he ain't been wearing his hearing aid.
(She opens a bottle of water and takes a tiny sip, carefully screwing the top back on.)
And here's the kicker – all that water out there? You can't drink <u>that</u> water!
(pointing off stage)

I've caught Baby lapping at the water around the house whenever I go out to check how things doing. I swat at her, but she pays me no mind. Dumb thing don't know any better. That's why I been trying to keep her in. Can't take no chance she gets into that cesspool again.
(Arranging and rearranging the bottles of water on the table.)

GLADYS (CONT.)

Got two bottles of pure drinking water left. Take real tiny sips to make it last. I just give Baby a tiny bit, few times a day. I try to explain, "We gots to make it last." But she don't understand. All she know is she's thirsty and why ain't I pouring more into her bowl? I can't do that, I say. But I know what she means. Wouldn't it be nice to guzzle a bottle down? Just pour it right on down my parched throat. That's the one thing that's dry around here – my throat. Don't that beat all!?
(She makes kissy sounds and listens, nothing, wipes sweat from her brow.)

Here's another crazy thought -- all this water ain't the only thing stinkin' up the place. Honey, I'm telling you, I could use a warm bath and a bar of soap. Maybe even add a little Calgon to the tub!
(She laughs then cuts herself off - pausing to listen.)

Hear it? Draining through my walls? Shh! Listen! Little rivers behind the photos of my granny, little rivers behind the Cuckoo clock, little rivers going-- where?

These last few nights I get in bed. Pull the damp sheet up against my moist skin, and I can hear Lake Ponchetrain at what was my front steps. Just begging to come in and get me like it done some my neighbors. Sometimes I actually fall asleep, but it ain't peaceful. And the dreams! My, Lord, the dreams! I'm on a ship at sea, 'cept this here boat ain't goin' nowhere. Stuck. Stuck in the middle of the wide blue ocean. Just -- stuck.

Last night I had a different dream. This time I was in a desert. The sun was baking my skin and it felt so good. There was sand beneath my feet, and the air was so crisp it felt like walking through crackers. There was ever so slight a breeze, like sandpaper against my cheeks. I didn't want to open my eyes, but even before I did, I could smell her. Baby, licking the salt off my face. Wet dog. Wet home. The wet. All around me. The sound of death is lapping at my doorstep. The smell of death is a wet smell.

GLADYS (CONT.)
Listen to me! All this morbid talk. Why, that? Out there?
That's just a big ole' mud puddle. It'll recede. You'll see. I
won't need no boat to get outta here, honey. Baby and me
gonna grab her leash and walk right down Napoleon when this
is all over. Mark my words. Walk right down Napoleon.

Baby? Baby, where you at? You don't think she got passed
me? I would have seen her, dontcha think? Baby? Come
here, honey, mama's gonna pour you a sip of water. Baby?
(She walks off stage.)

Baby? Baby?
*(She staggers back on stage, looks around the stage, grabs a bottle of water
and chugs it down as the lights fade.)*

THE END.

2 "NO ROOM AT THE CEMETERY"

from "Off the Map"
Anne -- in her late 70s, but she's in decent shape for her age and mobile.
Time: 2014
Place: Small Catholic cemetery near Bottineau, ND
(Anne props an arm up on a tombstone and raises her finger, as if it were a gun.)

ANNE
Dang! If I had Dad's laser rifle I could have gotten him. Put that laser on your target and it's lights out Mr. Gopher. Next time I'll bring the rifle. Crying shame what these gophers have done to the tombstones. Why look at this one, all cock-eyed and what not! Tsk-tsk. Darn gophers.
Well? Is this what you come to see? Tarsus. Population – zero. Though you can see -- we got plenty dead. But the dead don't pay taxes. So back in – oh, '90? '92? Something like that, the map makers out in Bismarck decided Tarsus didn't exist anymore. Poof! Off the Map. Tell that to them.
(gestures to the tombstones)

ANNE (CONT.)

This here is my husband Emory's grandparents – Henry and
Olivia Carbonneau. They're pleased to meet you.

Henry's parents homesteaded right over there. Then when he
was 31 his mother said, Henry, I'm sending you to Montreal to
find a wife. Don't come back till you got one. Turned out the
cousins he was staying with had an old maid cousin of their
own, Olivia. She was 26. Not much of a looker, but then
neither was Henry. When Henry came back to Tarsus he
brought Olivia and eventually they bought the land over there.

Let me introduce you to a few more folks. Over – oh, will you
look at the damage those badgers are doing to this place? This
gravestone looks like its been drinking. Tsk-tsk. Yep, Dad's
laser will do the trick.

Okay, then, so here we have . . . Milton Tousaint, born 1877,
died February 1907, and his wife Charlotte Tousaint, died
November, 1906. And then there's the baby, died 1909. Ah,
yes! This was a tragedy.

Charlotte got an infection after the baby was born, so she went
into the hospital in Bottineau. And Milton, he took his horse
into town to be near them, but he refused to get a room.
Cheapskate, he was. He told the stable manager, "I'll just bed
down with my horse." Stable manager says, "You'll catch your
death, it's November, man!"

But Milton, here, he was stubborn. Sure enough, the wife ends
up dying in the hospital and three months later Milton goes,
too. Pneumonia. The baby went to live with a sister, and she
was dead within 3 years. Tsk tsk. Tragic it was. The moral of
the story? Don't be a cheapskate!

Oh, my dat wind is wicked today! You know what they say,
North Dakota has Canada's topsoil, and South Dakota has
ours. Oh, ya, dat's an old one!

ANNE (CONT.)

Oh, and this one? Heffinfinger? He was a ne'r do well. Oh, ya! Church wouldn't let the family bury him in the cemetery. But when they moved the fence back in the 50s? He snuck in. My Emory -- he's in the nursing home now, that was our farm over there – see the Evergreens? We planted them in 1965. Yah. Emory. My Emory, such a handsome fella when I met him – still got the bluest eyes I ever seen. I wasn't the prettiest girl, but that day in the drug store he picked me. Oh, you should have seen the looks on the rich girls faces when he asked me to take a ride in his new Plymouth. Green with envy. *(Beat)*
I tried to keep Emory home, I did -- but it was too much after he caught that old timer's disease. When we took him to the nursing home he told the nurse, "She's sick of me now". Those were his words: "She's sick of me now." 'Bout broke my heart. Been married to that man for 60 years and we haven't written our last chapter yet.

Anyhow, Emory wants to be buried here in Tarsus, but the cemetery board tells me they ain't allowing any more burials. Not enough space, they say. Uff da, dat's all there is out here – space. True, there are a lot of unmarked graves. See, over in that there corner? I hear that's where they buried the unbaptized babies. But I don't know that for sure. That's just what they say. The cemetery keeper said that he's not digging any new graves 'cause he doesn't want to hit old bones. I wrote a letter but they completely misunderstood me. I just want to bury my husband with his people, where he belongs. *(shrugs, returns to the Carboneau grave)*

I guess I'll just have to do it myself if they won't do it for me. When Emory dies, I plan to have him cremated. I'll dig a hole over there by that there plum tree. A small hole for a big man. The cemetery board won't never know he's there. But I will, and I think, somehow, Emory will, too.

THE END.

3 "MARGE"

from *St. Bette's*

Time: 1961
Place: St. Elizabeth's - a home in Northern Minnesota for "unwed mothers"

Marge — late teens. She is quite close to full-term. She's a spirited young woman, does not fit the lady-like guidelines of the time, and this is her second baby she's releasing for adoption. In the old days, Marge would be a girl who'd "been around the block" — a few times.

Marge is lounging on her bed in the dorm room talking to her roommates.

MARGE
But, hey, don't they usually? Force us to have sex? If you do what they taught us -- say no -- the boy has no choice but to force you. He's gonna get what he wants, he's a boy, so how else can he unless he forces you and you pretend to be forced? What did the parents tell you? No parking, no petting, but be polite about it?
(male voice)
 "Care for some dick, ma'am?"
(Southern Belle voice)
"Why, no thank you, sir."

MARGE (CONT.)
(Parental Authority voice)
"The only birth control you need, dear, is an aspirin between your knees."
(natural voice)
Now, hold it there. Be firm, be pure, save it for your husband, ladies. Say, "No!" But the boy says, "Yes, oh, yes, honey, baby, sweetheart, I won't tell anyone," and "It won't hurt." Oh, and the biggest lie of all: "I'll pull out."

We say, "no, I shouldn't, I couldn't, I wouldn't," and "good girls don't" or "I'll get pregnant." But he's kissing those objections away, and soon our skirts are up, our panties are down, and by gosh, he's riding us! And we want it, too, because it feels good – that's what your mother will never tell you! And before we know it, girls, we're wrapping our legs around him, pulling him close, saying, "yes, oh, yes, baby, give it to me, give it to me!" Geez Louise!

Am I wrong, then? That's not how it happened with you? You weren't begging him in the end?
(pause)
Oh, you were *in love*. That's what all the "nice" girls say. They'll never admit that things got hot and heavy in the back seat of their boyfriend's Plymouth. That they were just plain old horny after the dance. Just like they won't admit to masturbating or farting. No, they were *in love*.

And then when you find out you're pregnant, it's like "How could this happen to little ole' me?" You had plans, you were going to go to secretarial school, learn steno, take your boss's dic-tation. Oh, no, you're not ready to be a mother!

So, you go, crying to Mummy, and she says she'll tell Daddy for you, but you know you're about to break his heart, you bad, bad girl. After all, if he couldn't touch you, nobody else was supposed to. So, you wait, wait for them to tell you how they're going to fix your little – problem. Will there be a shotgun wedding?

MARGE (CONT.)

Or maybe Daddy knows someone who can "take care of things"? Wink, wink. You wonder as you sit in the family den surrounded by your tidy middle-class life. Then they come in to tell you your fate.

Mummy's mascara is smeared. Daddy's eyes are red. And you're holding your breath. Here it is. The life-altering moment. Whatever their decision, you know you'll swallow it. You've learned to swallow -*(smiling)* and like it, too.

"You've been a very naughty girl," they say. "But we've called St. Bette's and there's a bed for you. And when you come home, we'll put this whole nasty episode behind us, dear."
Mom wipes your tears, but Daddy refuses to look you in the eye. His little girl is soiled now. She'll never be the same.
(looks at audience members)

That how it went? I'm close, ain't I? God, you're all such a clichés!

THE END.

4 "PLANTANOS"
a monologue

Sue - mid-50s, is your average, white, middle-class housewife with a secret affinity for exotic vegetables & fruits.

Time: Present
Place: Her kitchen counter. She will need a chopping board, knife, frying pan, an egg timer, cooking oil, a potato and a plantain.

SUE
(in deep voice)
"What's for dinner, Sue?"
(regular voice)
That's what my husband of 35 years says whenever he walks in the door. "What's for dinner, Sue?" And if there's no meat? Well, then it's not "dinner". He'll find a slab of frozen beef in the freezer and toss it in a pan. "A man needs meat, Sue It's in our DNA."

Meat and potatoes. It's been meat and potatoes every night of our marriage. Oh, meat and potatoes can be very -- filling. But it's possible to be full and not satisfied. I'm simply saying a woman needs variety in her diet. Bread, butter, mac and cheese, they're – dependable, predictable
(holds up potato) -- and that's why they're comfort foods. But let's admit it, ladies, a bit bland. Sometimes you get tired of vanilla and want a taste of mango.

SUE (CONT.)
(holds up a huge plantain)
I guess I was just in that kind of adventuress mood when I
was visiting my sister Betty in Miami. That's when she
introduced me to him -- I mean -- it. And that first time,
well, I felt like a girl again! It was like my taste buds woke up
and said, "Susie, where the hell you been keeping this baby?"
So, I brought one home in my suitcase and cooked it up for
Howard, thought I'd jazz things up a bit. But Howard? He
didn't get it. He asked, "Where's the mashed potatoes, Suse?"
The plantain was wasted on Howard. So now? It's been my
own secret pleasure for months.

I see that look in your eye. You're bored with rice and
potatoes. Pasta just doesn't pop like it did? I've been there.
So? What's the harm with a little – experimentation? No one
has to know. It'll be between you and your produce guy.

First, you have to find a very large, plantain. The blacker, the
longer, the better. Hey! You! We're talking produce here.
(Girl doesn't get out much, does she?)
Speaking of small towns, good luck if you're at a white bread
grocer. "Excuse me, sir, where are your plantains?"
(exaggerated Southern accent)

"My plan-tations? Why, sugar, my great-grandpappy lost that
after the Northern invasion."

Or try to find some malanga. Ma-lan-ga? Thick, brown,
hairy. It's a *root* vegetable, honey. You mash it. Oh, and
there are so many exotic fruits out there for you to try –
elephant fruit, and ugly fruit, one bite and the sticky juice will
run down your chin – oh, my! Is it hot in here or is it just
me?

Okay, so let's say you find a nice, long plantain at your A&P,
grab it before another hungry woman does. You want one
that's not green. If it's green you'll have to be patient.

SUE (CONT.)

And maybe <u>you're</u> patient when it comes to your satisfaction, but me? Please. Anticipation is one thing, but I need my sleep! And the older Howard gets, the more patience I need. Anyway, what you're looking for is a ripe plantain. Kinda like the over-ripe bananas they mark down for a quick sale? Except you're not looking for an itty bitty banana. <u>You</u> want a handsome, mature plantain.

If you're lucky enough to find one, put that baby in your cart and bring'em on home. This can get messy, so best to slip on an apron -- panties are optional.
(she puts on a little frilly thing)
Pour some cooking oil in a frying pan and wait for it to sizzle. While things are heating up, take a good look at your plantain. Run a gentle finger across its skin. Isn't it smooth? Ripe but, still firm. Yes, it's true: it's a little ugly. Maybe you'll begin to wonder, do I really want to try this? What would my friends think?

Push aside these questions. First timer flutters. Squash those inhibitions and pick up that plantain, woman. Peel back the skin. Gently, now, lay it on your cutting board, find a sharp knife and after a small prayer of thanks to the God who creates all things, slice. There will be little resistance, and you could chop, chop, chop, but what's the pleasure in that? Take your time, move your blade on a diagonal a centimeter thick. Enjoy the sensation of the stainless steel sliding through the soft fruit. One, two, three, four, five, ummmm. A large plantain? Who knows how many slices you'll enjoy.

So? Is your oil hot enough, yet? Good. Set the timer for a minute.
(does so — you will need to time out the following)
Carefully pick up the sliced plantain and put it in the oil. It may pop as the moist flesh hits the grease, but it will soon settle into a nice low sizzle. Turn down the heat, just a tad. Some things shouldn't be rushed. Find your spatula. I like a metal one.

SUE (CONT.)
(She holds one up and slaps her bottom.)
In a few minutes, depending on the intensity of the heat, you'll want to flip them. Then you'll do the same thing on the other side. They should be golden brown. And the smell! Heaven. Sweet, fried, crispy, yummy.

You're anticipation will begin to climax at this point. Take a deep breath, find a plate, put down a paper towel to absorb the oil and think of Cuba: Turquoise ocean, soft white sand, the sound of palm fronds rattle in a soft breeze. A tall, dark stranger rising out of the ocean in a red Speedo strolls towards you. Droplets of water glisten off his sleek Adonis body. His lips part to reveal perfect, white teeth in a tan face. Bottomless brown eyes twinkle. He kneels, placing one rippling arm on either side of your shoulders. His eyes move to your mouth, you taste salt as water trails off his black, wavy hair onto your lips. He leans in with those thick, luscious –
(Timer goes off.)
Oh! Your plantains are done! Better lift them out before they go from golden to burnt. Drain, cool, not too much, and fill your plate. Crispy on the outside, soft, sweet meat on the inside. Except it's not meat. It's a plantano. And it – is delicious.

THE END.

5 "IT'S FOR THE BEST"

from St. Bette's

Sister Anne - 30s up to mid-50s, is a nun. While she is stern, she is not unfeeling, nor is she a stereotype. She has come to see a resident, Marge, who has recently delivered and has second thoughts about releasing her child for adoption.

Time: Summer, 1961

Place: Dorm room in St. Bette's, a home for unwed mothers, in northern Minnesota.

SISTER ANNE
The first day is the hardest. What you're feeling right now, many other girls felt. You're confused. You're doubting your decision. But that's today. Tomorrow, or the next day you'll realize that your initial decision was the right one. Margaret? Don't get all soft on me, not now. You made your choices, now live by them. What you're experiencing now is simply baby blues. A week from now you'll be glad you gave her up.

SISTER ANNE (CONT.)

A long time ago, there was a girl, a head strong girl, not unlike yourself. She came to a place like this, prepared to give up her baby. But at the last moment, she changed her mind. That girl broke hearts. The heart of the woman who could not have a baby but who thought she was about to get one. The heart of the man who expected to walk away with a child to care and protect.

But that girl, that girl did not care whose lives she destroyed. She only cared about herself and what she wanted in that moment, never looking ahead, but what she wanted in that instant, how she felt at that moment. She left, took her baby and a month later, when she couldn't feed herself, couldn't care for the baby, she returned to the home.

The sisters took the baby back, of course, but this time she had to hand her child over and it was twenty times, no one hundred times more difficult. It felt like one of her limbs was being torn from her body. It was for the best, of course; it's always for the best, but it was so much harder than it needed to be. But that's how this girl was. Hard headed. Always found the most difficult route to travel. Marge, you remind me of this girl. Do yourself and everyone else a favor, take the more direct route this time. Believe me, it's for the best.

THE END.

6 "MILK DREAMS"

from *Milk Dreams*

Marie — mid-20s to mid-30s, has struggled throughout the play with learning to breast feed her first child. Once she learned the "how" she confronted societal stigmas relating to the "where" and "how long." In the following she comes into her own.

MARIE
That was it. I'd been humiliated in public. It was time to wean. People thought there was something immoral about my feeding my toddler with my body. I'm sure some people thought I must be getting some sort of erotic kick. (*Shudders*) And they thought *I* was perverted. That night when I nursed my daughter, she did what she always did as she fell asleep, she patted my chest. This tiny, innocent looking hand, safe in knowing she was in her mother's arms. She felt safe. I was so confused when I went to bed that night. And I dreamed, but this time it wasn't of the self-righteous chickens clucking in the barnyard. This time . . .

(*DRUMMING BEGINS SOFTLY.*)
It was one of those dreams when you're flying -- you know? The air was in my face, hair billowing behind me, gliding over rooftops, the whole bit. Then I kind of swooped down and there were these women, women of every shape, height, and color.

MARIE (CONT.)

Women sitting on benches in parks, by the sea, by the dessert, in the forests, on top of mountains, in front of office buildings, at bus stops, women nursing their babies. Then it was like the women got older, I mean not older as in their age, but older as in from *other* ages.

It was as if I were flying backward in time, and seeing women from the 19th century, the 18th, the 17th . . . ancient women with their babies, until there was this one woman who was bare breasted sitting in a clearing. Her baby cried and she put him to her breast. Her baby cried and she put him to her breast. Her baby cried -- and she put him to her breast.

I woke up the next morning with this incredible feeling of knowing that whatever I chose to do, continue breastfeeding my daughter until we were both ready to wean, or end this chapter in our relationship, no matter what – I was her mother and the choice I made would be based on what I felt was right for us. I am her mother.
(DRUMS CEASE.)
I get to choose.

I went into her room where she was sleeping. You know how their little faces are in slumber, all soft and relaxed? Then I saw her lips. They were moving. She was deep in sleep and having milk dreams. Dreams of deep satisfaction. I sat there until dawn and drank her image in.

THE END.

7 "CHOCOLATE"

from *Flesh & Bones*

Billi - 17-something on up through early 30s, overweight

Billi, an aspiring blues singer, has been rejected by a director due her "image" -- she's over weight. She has been holed up in her apartment for a week eating Ring Dings and Fritos. Her best friend, Liz, a closet bulimic, has just stopped by to encourage her to lose weight and the director will reconsider her for the lead in an upcoming musical.

BILLI

Excuse me? Give up *chocolate*? Chocolate? Don't you see what you're asking me? You're asking me to give up the one constant in my life. The one dependable support system in this damned, unpredictable world? You act like this is some small modification, like closing the toilet seat. This is a colossal alteration of the very fiber of my being. Why not just take me out and shoot me? That would be humane. That – would be merciful. See, to you it's just a simple matter of never eating chocolate again. To renounce its existence and turn a treasonous tongue towards low cal, saccharine soaked sweeties. And don't you start talking health food, 'cause in an emotional crunch, carob just don't cut it!

Look, what you don't understand is the rich history chocolate and I have. It isn't just so much cocoa and corn syrup. It's spiritual sustenance, too. Chocolate and I go way back.

BILLI (CONT.)
It was over hot fudge sundaes that Debbie Pulaski comforted me after my first break up with Larry Sullivan. It was with double fudge cake that you relayed the news that Debbie was dating Larry.

And it was during a fudge making party that you, Debbie and I celebrated the triumph of sisterhood ---- and the dumping of Larry. I could tell you stories of pot brownies and hot August nights with melted Hershey's kisses, but why get into it? Suffice it to say, if you take away my chocolate – I --will -- die. Or at least suffer severe DTs I guarantee: it won't be pretty.

THE END.

8 "ALL BOW TO THE GODDESS OF THIN"

from *Flesh & Bones*

LIZ – 17 up to early 30s, bulimic

Liz is at a diner smoking a cigarette and eating a house salad with a glass of water. Her own dieting compulsion has gotten way out of hand at this point.

LIZ
Billi? I haven't seen her in a while. Ever since we went shopping. She's kind of a drag to be around lately. All we ever do is talk about what we've eaten that day. I can do that on my own. I do.

I guess you could say I'm kind of obsessive about food. I mean, I think about it *all* the time. Right now, I'm eyeballing that guy's double cheeseburger and my mouth is literally salivating. But I ordered a salad. No dressing. And a glass of water with ice –you burn more calories that way.

God, I'm always hungry. The soundtrack to my life is my stomach growling. But unlike Billi I can control myself.

LIZ (CONT.)
Sure, sometimes I get a little crazy and eat too much, but I take care of it. I know it sounds insane, but I can't let all that food stay in my body! That's even grosser than what I do. Look at Billi. I love her to death; she's my best friend, but God! You've seen her! She doesn't eat; she inhales!

When we were kids, I was the fat one. But now she's the one who's totally out of control. Although, I must confess that most of the times we go out to eat it is my idea. I find myself fascinated with the experience, like it's a lab experiment. What will she order? And will she go for dessert, too? I guess you could say I get a vicarious kick out of watching her chow down. Not just 'cause I wish I could eat the food, but more because I look at her and think, "She can't resist. No self-discipline." And I know that I have it all under control. *(Takes a deep drag on her cigarette).*
Sometimes, though, I can go way overboard, too, but I got it figured out. Purging ain't pretty, but a girl's got to do what a girl's got to do.

There are times when I can get pretty depressed about my little habit. I mean, sure, I know it's not the healthiest way to go, but really? What choice do I have? Laxatives of course, but they're not always convenient. They're great on weekends, though. Last Friday, some of the girls wanted to do happy hour. And I ate like a pig! Well, Saturday I just popped a bunch of Ex-lax and – oh, don't make that face! You *wish* you had my discipline. I've got ten pounds to lose before this big interview on Thursday. That's only five days away. Impossible? Just watch and see. Then – eat your heart out, bitches.

THE END.

9 "NO PAIN, NO GAIN"
From *Flesh & Bones*

Darla - twenties, an aerobics instructor. She's got what's often called a "hard body" — no fat just lean muscle.

Darla has just passed Liz on her way into the diner.

DARLA
Geez! Did you get a load of the attitude on that bitch?
B-r-r-r! Like sub-zero! Wow, like I know they're jealous of
me, and they've got good reason, but it's just not fair. I
mean, they act like I was born with a great body, like it was
some sort of gift! Sure, I do have good genes on both sides,
but, listen, I work on it, too. 'Specially the honey. I mean
this thing can get way out of control if I so much as skip
one single day. Which I rarely do. See, I teach Zhumba
five days a week? And work out with weights every other
day? I don't see those girls on Saturday or Sunday doing
abdominal crunches and pectoral squeezes. No, they're
probably still nice and comfy under the covers scarfing
down some –
(this is pure porn for her)
-- big, buttery, flakey croissant slathered with jam, possibly
Nuttella – oh, yes, Nuttella, and a cup of coffee with real

DARLA (CONT.)
-- cream and sugar, oh, no a Mocha latte, oooooooooooh yeah.
(Shakes herself out of the fantasy.)
Or if they <u>were</u> able to get their lazy hineys out of bed, they're having some fattening champagne brunch somewhere, never even giving a second thought to the salad table, nope, goin' straight for the carbs. Will they choose pancakes, waffles, or French toast? Aw, hell, they'll take them all. Greedy little carb monsters. Not to mention some greasy sausage AND fatty bacon. Will they stop there? Oh, no. They'll need a sugar chaser after the protein, so they'll waddle on back and their pudgy little hearts will beat ever so much faster at the sight of muffins, cakes and cookies.
(falling into the fantasy of it, again)

Cheese Danish that's so creamy, and sticky you just gotta lick each and every finger. Ummm . . .

No self-discipline. They'll wash it all down with another Mimosa and later cry, "Why am I so fat?" Pathetic.

But hey, I don't like to judge. I'm no diet freak or anything. No, I'm pretty lucky on account of my fast metabolism. Fact is, I *could* eat just 'bout anything I want. Don't you just hate me?

The thing is, half the time I forget to eat. I'm busy working out, or teaching Zumba, or working out. Not that I don't have a life!

No, I'm married. Me and Jeff, that's my hubby, when we're not working out together, we like to go for long bike rides. Or we jog together. I love my life just the way it is, which is why I got so mad the other day when Jeff wanted me to get rid of my birth control.

DARLA (CONT.)
Like I really want to have a baby after all the work I've put into this bod?

Geez! I mean you get stretch marks! Not to mention your waist is never the same. Let's not even think about the boobs. Ughh! But Jeff doesn't understand. Men never do. He actually said I've got my priorities mixed up. Like he didn't marry me for my body? I'm no genius, but I can figure that one out. But now HE wants a baby. Says there's something missing in OUR lives. I said, yeah, baby, a home gym. Then he has the nerve to call me vain! Like that's a *bad* thing?

If this was about him getting preggers, I guarantee we'd be talking to adoption agencies like yesterday. Geez! Excuse me, waiter? A house salad, please, extra lettuce. See? I have no problem with food.

THE END.

10 "THICK THIGHS ANONYMOUS"

from *Flesh & Bones*

Tracy G. – 20s on up, she's big, she's bold, and she is a divine diva

There is an audience plant required. She has one word: "Fat."

It's a T.T.A. meeting (Thick Thighs Anonymous) - all that's required is a podium with a sign. Your audience is the meeting's membership. Tracy G. makes a grand entrance, commanding the audience's attention.

TRACY G.
Good evening everyone and welcome to the first session of T.T.A. I'm Tracy G., and I'll be your group leader. Why don't we get right to the point, shall we? I firmly believe that the direct approach is the best approach. So, why beat around the bush? No use in putting off to tomorrow what you can do today, Why not just jump right in? After all, she who hesitates is lost. So, lets grab the bull by the horns. Yes?

You're here tonight to talk about---the "T" word. I realize that most of you hate to even think about it, much less discuss it in a public forum such as this, --

TRACY G. (CONT.)

--but the time has come! Out! I say! Venture forth into the brightness of day and say it loud, say it strong!

Together ladies and gentlemen, together in one glorious union, together on the count of three!

Take a deep breath--one, and with pride -- two, and with dignity -- three! THIGHS!!!

Oh my, well, that wasn't very nice of you, now was it?

Well, perhaps you haven't arrived yet, but you shall. By the end of this meeting you may only be able to get out the "th," yes, maybe just the "th," but that "th" will be ever so significant. And next time, if you apply yourself, you may be able to get in the "I," and really, what could be simpler than a "th," and an "I"? It's not like we're a support group for that "D" word -- derriere, dear.

Heavens no! We're way past that point. And from here, why it's just a hop, skip, and a jump to calves and ankles, and from there what's left, but the toes. And toes very rarely give anyone any trouble. That is -- if you have all ten. If you don't, I know of a very good toe support group, which meets on alternate Tuesdays and Thursdays. Talk to me later. Back to the issue at hand. Thighs.

Do your shirt tops come below your knees? Do you hide your thighs beneath yards of fabric, smothering their skin, stifling their spirit? You do, don't you? I see you out there, you thigh stiflers! You who stay away from cropped tops, who never tuck in your shirts, who only dare wear Bermuda shorts in summer and only on the most sweltering of days. I see you, and I am here to tell you, you will be thigh shy –

TRACY G. (CONT.)
-- no more! I will venture to add that you will even learn to love your thighs! Yes, love them!

You've tried ellipticals, and step aerobics, you've tried saunas, lotions, and herbal wraps, now try love my friends!

The first step is touching those mighty thighs. Come on now: Really touch them. You've pinched them and slapped them, but ah! Have you touched them? Caressed them? What do they feel like? What do they really feel like?

BILLI
(in audience)
FAT!

TRACY G.
Fat?! Who said that?! You think they feel fat, do you? You think this entire organization is a crock of caca, don't you? Hundreds of dollars of research have gone into developing this program, but you think you have all the answers, do you? Well, let me ask you one thing, Miss Everything is a Crock of Caca: What is fat spelled backwards? Hmm? Taf. What's Taf? Is it in the dictionary? No, no, my friends. You will not find it in Webster's, because taf does not exist. Taf is a figment of your imagination. Dismiss taf right now, and with it fat.

Now, if your thighs cannot feel FAT what can they feel? Hmm? Soft perhaps? Warm, cushy? Why I bet they're strong, too. Aren't they? I bet they could crush a man's head like a walnut!

Now, I want you to lean over, that's right. Don't be thigh shy. Lean over and grab those meaty thighs and tell them you love them. And don't just say it. Really mean it! Go on, now.

TRACY G. (CONT.)
What's this whispering about?
You can do better than that!

Okay, okay, work on it then. For your thigh work you are to stand in front of the mirror, completely naked and address your thighs. Don't forget the extra postage. Ha, ha!

No, ahem, you tell your thighs how happy you are to have them in your life, and that your lower legs would be nowhere without them.

Okay, well that's all for this evening's session of Thick Thighs Anonymous. There are cookies and cake at the back of the room.

Mingle, everyone, mingle! Revel in the mighty thunder of thighs against thighs! Ta-ta!

THE END.

11 "PULLING OUT ALL THE STOPS"

a monologue

Jane — late 30s up to late-40s (just change the age when required in the monologue)

Jane is seated at her vanity, "putting on her face." She has a bottle of opened champagne and a half-filled glass in front of her. Her cat is asleep next to her. Her friend Loraine has stopped by. It is New Year's Eve.

JANE
Hey, Loraine! Come on in! <u>You</u> look gorgeous! Have a seat, hon, this shouldn't take me too much longer. Help yourself to the champagne. Don't you just love Cold Duck?

Love the hair! Where'd you get it done? *(pause)* Cost Cutters? No, they do a good job. Depends on the girl you get, but, sure, they do good work. Me? I went to Penny's. Yeah. I know, I know they're a bit spendy, but sometimes you gotta pull out all the stops, know what I'm saying?

That's my motto for 20-__, Loraine: Pull Out All the Stops. I mean, I have to face it: I'm 44 years old, Loraine. It's true. And there aren't too many more shopping days 'til Xmas, hear what I'm saying? My eggs got an expiration date, Loraine, and if I'm gonna use 'em before they go bad I gotta get fryin'.

JANE (CONT.)
In 201_ I am gonna find me Mr. Right, Loraine. Oh, sure, I've gotten close but not Mr. Right. I keep getting drawn to Mr. Unavailable.

Remember Charlie? Very cute but also very married. Maybe that's where my bad karma started.

Then there was Gary. He seemed to have it all goin' on: good sense of humor, good job, good head of hair. But then he took me home to meet his mother. And then I realized he took me home to meet his mother. He lived with his mother. And he wasn't looking to move out. Thought we could shack up in her basement. Why not, he said? It's finished. Then I find out that wherever he goes, his mother goes. When he invited her on our romantic trip to the Poconos, that was it. I ain't sharing a bed with nobody's mother, even if it is heart-shaped. Sigh-o-nara, Gary.

After Gary there was Harold. *(sighs)* Harold was a one-woman man. Not married. Large – income. A CPA. His mother was dead. Very nice. But Harold didn't have -- What do you call it? Social skills. No ability to carry on his half of the conversation. I mean, I like to talk, but dating Harold was like talking to myself. Even my cat has more facial expression. Isn't that right, Chaka Khan?
(strokes kitty)
Once, we went to dinner and after I got tired of trying to make conversation for like an hour, I kind of zoned off. When he asked me to pass the catsup I practically jumped out of my skin! I'd forgotten I was with someone!

No, I've had it with the Charlies, Garys, and Harolds of the world. This year is the year, Loraine. Not only did I get my hair done at Penny's I had my moustache waxed. Yep. No more bleaching for this girl. I mean, I'm __ years old, Loraine. I gotta step it up.
(confidentially)

JANE (CONT.)
And -- I did me a little post-Christmas shopping and decided to finally find out exactly what Victoria's secret is. And now I know, Loraine! Now, I know! I bought me a thong! But after I put it on I realized I still needed my girdle. Do you think wearing a girdle over a thong defeats the purpose?

Oh, and I bought me some fancy perfume -- off the pretty girl at the cosmetic counter. No more magazine samplers for me. Oh, and a fresh lipstick.
(sighs as she produces a new lipstick)
Anything seems possible with a fresh lipstick.

20__ is gonna be my year, Loraine. I can feel it in my bones. No more catch and release. No more crying over the one that got away. This year I'm hauling in the big one. That's it, Loraine! I been fishing with all the wrong bait. You don't use a worm to catch a trout. You gotta use the best push-up bra money can buy! Because this year, Loraine, this year I'm hookin' Mr. Right. And after I net 'em I'm gonna stuff 'em and mount 'em. He's not wigglin' away from me this time. No sir, this year I'm getting me a keeper. And then, and only then will I take off my girdle. Cause this year, Loraine? I'm pullin' out <u>all</u> the stops!

(Puts on a big pair of thick lensed glasses, then takes a sip of her champagne)

Oo, that tickles!

THE END.

12 "BRA-VO!"

a monologue

Time: Present.

Place: Ladies fitting room in department store. Molly has "three sheets to the wind," as they say, and is sipping on a flask. She has a tape measure hanging around her neck.

Molly – 20s on up. She's had a nip or two.

MOLLY
(in middle of taking a sip from a small flask)
Oh, you startled me! *(pause)* No, no, no. I was just taking my coffee break,
(Tucks flask in her bra.)
Come into my dressing room. My name is Molly, Ill be your Mit Fistress. I mean your Fit Mistress. Brassieres are my specialty. If they gave PhDs in Bra History, you would have to call me Dr. Molly. Did you know that brassiere is French for "upper arm" – 'cept in America we don't wear 'em on our upper arms. We wear 'em on our tits! Ha!

MOLLY (CONT.)
Oops. I mean breasts. Management doesn't like me to call 'em tits or boobs, but over the last year I've heard women refer to them as all sorts of things including Bouncing Berty and –Bodacious tatas. Let's see, there's ... bazookas, bazongas, torpedoes, gazongas, desk, rack, knockers, honkers, hooters, boobies, floaters, coconuts, cupcakes, melons, peaches, headlights, Chi Chis, twin peaks, mamms, mosquito bites, milk jugs, lactation stations and Dick squeezer. But I like to refer to them as – "the girls".

What's a matter? Where you going? I'm a professional, not gonna bite! I'm here to make your life -- fuller. *(giggles)*

Did you know that 10 out 6 women are wearing the wrong bra? It's true. Oprah said so. She also said that a good bra can make all the difference in the world!

What's that? Can it what? Solve world hunger? No, hon, it's just a bra – you want a miracle bra? Ha! You gotta go to that fancy pants underwear store in the mall. This here's Sears, sister.

Okay, off with it, I got a line out there all the way to housewares. Buy two get one free. So? Off with your top!

Aw! You're blushing. Nothing to be embarrassed by, you don't got anything I haven't seen before. Big, small, perky, floppy – hairy moles -- nothing surprises me since I saw that one with the witch's tit. A witch's tit? That's when you got a third one, right in the middle. Yep, had a nipple growing right here. Triple the pleasure? I wouldn't know. Hey, it happens. You don't have a witch's tit, do you? Nothing to be shy about, then; off with it.

MOLLY (CONT.)
(looks away, but cuts her eyes over – peeking)
What was all your fussin' about? You really could get by with a nice little cami. On sale: 3 for $15.

Okay, fine then. Arms up –
(taking off tape measure around her neck, miming measuring a woman)

– uh – huh *(giggles)* and out – uh – huh – uh -huh. You want the good news or the bad news first?

The good news is we <u>do</u> have a bra in your size. The bad news is -- they're not any cheaper just cause they're smaller. Ha!

Sorry, just a little booby humor. <u>Little</u> booby – get it? Comes with the job. Okay, now, do you know how to put a bra on?
(all serious and professional now, as if the following has been memorized)
Lesson number one: When you put your bra on, slip the straps over your shoulders, like so, then drop over from the waist -- come on, do it with me, that's right. You drop over from your waist and touch your toes. Ha! I'm pulling your leg!
(back to her professional voice)
Lesson number two: Lean forward and fill those cups -- go on and fill'er up. If you can't fill 'er up your cups are too big for your girls and you need a smaller size. If your girls are too big, your cup over floweth, and you need a larger cup – perhaps a jug! Ha!

MOLLY (CONT.)
(professional voice)
Now, stand up and adjust the breasts -- no you gotta jiggle them around so they settle in nice and snug. Like two cooing doves each in her own nest Can you hear them? Coo coo. Coo coo.
Perfect. Except, not so perfect. But it's okay. A lot of women have one girl larger than the other. Nothing to be self conscious about. Why, I can hardly tell your left one is larger. Oh, usually it's the left, don't ask me why, it's just the left. You'd think it'd be the right since most people are righties, but no, it's the left. Just like yours!
(transitioning into professional voice)
A-hem. Lesson number three: If you have one girl obviously larger than the other, loosen the bra strap on the larger one. And always, always fit the cup size to the larger girl first.

What's that? Why, of course, you'll take it. It's going to change your life. Who cares if it's $75 on sale? Unlike all those women walking around out there, you've been fitted by a professional and now you've got a bra that fits your titties. Sorry, did I say titties? I meant "girls." Fits your girls right. Fits your *soul.*

Wait, don't go yet! Lesson number three or is it four? If your bra rides up in the back, adjust the straps to a comfortable length. Or try hooking your bra more snuggly so it fits better. And if you have back fat, we have a bra for that, too. Why there's one to minimize, to maximize, to wear with a strapless or a plunging neckline, to hide those pesky nipples, or let them show – if you're that kinda girl. And they come in every color – one for every outfit, everyday and night of the week! Wait! I'm not done! I have much more bra wisdom for you! Have wrinkly cups?

MOLLY (CONT.)
Then the cups are too big for your girls. You may need a smaller size. Cups should contain each breast completely and fit smoothly. Got questions? Just come on back and ask for me, Molly the Fit Mistress. Next!
(arching her back, she tugs at her bra)

Oh, god is it time to go home? This thing is killing me!
(removes bra)

THE END.

13 "Right as Rain"
from "Ralph's Ark"

MAGGIE, a 40-ish mother of two teenagers and the wife of Ralph, who has had a mental breakdown due to the loss of the family farm, is in complete denial about her family. She cleans to try to bring order to their lives. Her daughter, Denise, has called in a Catholic priest (even though they're not Catholic) to help counsel the family and get them the help they need.

MAGGIE

I cannot believe she left you a message. Denise! You left a message?! Why didn't you just go down to the café and tell the town you think our family is in trouble? Don't mind Denise. She's melodramatic. I have my job, and her father has his - - project. And she's obviously hungry for a little attention. There is nothing so terribly strange about building an ark in one's yard. Lots of people get carried away with things. Why, my Aunt Susan loved pigs. She had pictures and little knick-knacks of pigs all over her house. Ceramic pigs, fabric pigs, why even a velvet painting of a pig dressed as Elvis! Even had them in the bathroom!

MAGGIE (CONT.)

And when you opened her refrigerator to get, oh say a slab of *bacon*, there was a plastic pig in there that oinked at you. It did! You've heard of people like that, haven't you, Father? My, it's strange calling you that – Father. Why, you're young enough to be my son, maybe not my son because I would have been about ten when I had you, although, I once knew a girl who had a baby at twelve, so it's possible, still it's odd to keep calling you "Father" unless . . . my mother married a younger man, and then you could be my stepfather, in which case I might very well have to call you "father." But it would be strange.

Really, everything is just fine and dandy. Hunky dory. Super duper. I'm sorry you had to come all the way out here to drink my tea without real milk, and eat stale cookies, but every thing is just fine with our family. We are just as normal a family as you'd ever want to meet. Boring really. (yawns) So, you go on back to town and spread the word. In fact, go tell ole' Marge at the café. Tell'er you saw us and that the Hansons are just as right as rain!

THE END

14 "GO AWAY"

almost a monologue

Franny – 20s on up.

Man – about the same age if not older than Franny. Average looking.

Time: Right now.

Place: Bust station waiting room.

Franny rushes onto the stage as best she can while dragging several pieces of luggage. She looks frazzled and approaches an audience member.

FRANNY
Have I missed the bus? Any bus. I don't care where it's going – Butte, Missoula, Missouri, Mississippi – where ever – have I missed it?
(pause)
Oh, good. Look, would you mind looking after these, I'll stick them right over here – I just need to find out when the next bus is. Please? Okay, be right back.

(She exits briefly as bus arrivals are announced.)

V.O.

The 8:08 to Missoula will be arriving ten minutes late at Gate 6.
Repeat: The 8:08 to Missoula will be arriving ten minutes late at Gate
6. Ticketed passengers only.

FANNY

Hi, thank you so much! Looks like I'm going to Montana. Billings.
That's a big city, I think, right?

(She now carries a can of soda and some candy. She sits down on a chair or bench, closes her eyes for a beat, then opens a bag of M&M peanuts.)

I really appreciate you looking after my bags. Do you know there are
actually people who would say "no" to a request like that? There are,
believe me. "Don't involve me," they'd say. Or, simply, "Sorry," but
they're not, not the least bit sorry. They're just looking out for
themselves, their own interests, and that's not necessarily a bad thing,
is it? When I get to, where did I say I was going? Oh, yeah, when I
get to Billings, I'm going to do a whole lot more of looking out for
my best interests than I am other people's. Still, I do appreciate you
looking after my bags. Hey, want some?
(offers candy)
More for me then! Dinner of champions! Hey, at least they have
peanuts, peanuts are good for protein, right?
(she takes a long sip of her soda, relaxing, she looks around)
There's something very wrong with this picture isn't there? I look like
I'm running away from home. Fact is, I am. Irony is, I did this when
I was fourteen. But for Pete's sake, I'm ___! A ___-year old shouldn't
be packing up everything she can squeeze into her suitcase and
running away from home. But he just won't -- go away.
At first I didn't want him to go away. I met him at work. He was a
customer. He was charming. Ding-ding-ding. Right then and there I
should have heard the alarm bell going off. Beware of charming
individuals!

FRANNY (CONT.)

At first I didn't want him to go away. I met him at work. He was a customer. He was charming. Ding-ding-ding. Right then and there I should have heard the alarm bell going off. Beware of charming individuals! Why do they need to use charm, right? Why not just be them selves? What's with the hard sell? Either people are going to like them or not, but the charming stuff, that's like sugar-coating something, and why would you need to do that unless it was so ---distasteful you wanted to disguise it? Well, turns out he was distasteful, so distasteful I can't get the taste of him out of my mouth.

But I bought the charm, hook, line, and sinker. We went out on a few dates. And it was nice. I admit, I even thought he might be "the one." But then, when he had a fit when I wanted to spend time with my girlfriends, when I wasn't home exactly 30 minutes after work and he had a cow – I mean, who was this guy? I barely knew him? His charm began to quickly wear off, especially when he wouldn't stop calling. He called me at home, at work, when I got home from work. He was driving me crazy, so I told him I needed some space. Isn't that what anyone would do? Well, he didn't take it so well. At first he was hurt. And I felt guilty, but I just wanted a little breathing room, so I held firm. I'd see him at the end of the week. What was so wrong with that? But he wouldn't go away -- calling me, sending e-mails, flowers. The girls at work thought it was romantic, but for me – it was too much. Come on, it was creeping me out.

So, when Saturday came, I cancelled our date. That's when the charm totally slipped away. He wasn't hurt now. He was angry. He came over to my apartment, screaming, banging the door, begging I let him in.

FRANNY (CONT.)

I did, because I could hear the neighbors' sliding back their peep holes, you know that sound? Click, click, click. I was embarrassed, I just wanted him to calm down, thought I could get him to So, I let him in. Bad idea. He didn't calm down, he got angrier, he smashed this little dog figurine my grandmother had given me when I was eight. Then he smashed me. In the mouth. Nobody hits me. So I told him "leave or I'm calling the police." He left. For awhile. A week.

The phone messages started, long letters about how much I meant to him, how we were suppose to be together. He started selling the charm again, but this time I wasn't buying. I ignored him. This must have infuriated him, after all he was using his best material and it wasn't working. The phone messages stopped being all kissing, sweetie stuff, and started getting ugly. He'd swear on my answering machine, call me at work and when I told my co-workers not to put his calls through, he swore at them.

I was tense all the time: every time the phone rang I braced myself. One day it was him, and I gave it to him, told him to go away. Leave me alone. I came out of work that day and found all four of my tires slashed. I called the police, and this time I got a restraining order.

Funny thing, we think a little piece of paper will make us safe. Maybe for some it does, but not me. I never felt safe. He stopped calling me, yes, stopped following me, but there were signs he'd been around A single rose petal by the front of my door, an empty can of Coke in my car that I hadn't drunk. Little signs that he'd been where he shouldn't have, but most of the time I couldn't put my finger on it. Things had been moved just slightly. I couldn't prove it, oh, but I knew he'd been around.

FRANNY (CONT.)
It was making me crazy, and the police couldn't help. He
wasn't coming by, he wasn't calling, what did I want them to
do? I wanted them to make him go away. But they
couldn't.

Then . . . this morning I woke up, feeling kind of groggier
than usual, and I went into my bathroom. I live by myself.
And the toilet seat was up. You know, the bottom ring, like
men do when they have to pee? It was up. I backed out of
that bathroom, ran into my bedroom, locked the door, then
I thought – he's in here! He's in my bedroom. Was he in
the closet? Under my bed? Behind the curtains? I grabbed
the first thing I could put my hands on, some sweats and
dressed with my back against my bedroom door.

I waited. I listened. I'd think I heard something beyond my
bedroom door. I can tell you that my heart was about to
bust out of my chest. Finally, I decided I'd make a run for
it. I opened the door, ran for the front hall, grabbed the
only shoes that were sitting there, a pair of black pumps and
my purse, and I ran to the police station. I must have
looked like a crazy lady in baggy sweats and pumps, and
when I got a cop to go back to my apartment with me, he
treated me like I was crazy.

"But the toilet seat is up! He was in here!" Was there any
sign of breaking and entering? No, no sign. Had I given him
a key? No, but he could have easily gotten hold of mine and
made a copy. Now I sounded paranoid, I am paranoid, but
with good reason, don't you think? He left the toilet seat up.
That was a message: "I can come and go in your life and you
can't do anything about it."

FRANNY (CONT.)
"But the toilet seat is up! He was in here!" Was there any sign of
breaking and entering? No, no sign. "But the toilet seat is up! " Had
I given him a key? No, but he could have easily gotten hold of mine
and made a copy. Now I sounded paranoid, I am paranoid, but with
good reason, don't you think? He left the toilet seat up. That was a
message: "I can come and go in your life and you can't do anything
about it."

I was crying, begging the officer, "Please, make him go away!" He
looked a little frustrated, and then he said, sometimes the only thing
to do in these situations is for the victim to go away. Is there
anywhere you can go, anyone you can visit until he forgets about you?
I wish there were. There isn't. But I knew right then that he wasn't
going to leave me alone if I stayed in this town. So, I made the police
officer wait while I threw anything that was important enough to take
into these bags.

I'm 30 years old and I'm running away from home. But, hey, there's
my bus. I gotta go, start over, new town, new job, I don't know what
awaits me in Billings, but I know one thing that won't be there: Him.
Hey, take care.
(*She exits with her suitcase. A man enters, holding a driver's license.*)

MAN
Hey, did you see a woman, brown hair, about 5'5"? I think I found
her driver's license.

THE END.

15 "You Have a Baby?

from Compañeras

Time: Mid-1970s

Place: Punta de Rieles Women's Prison; Montevideo, Uruguay

The following monologue is spoken directly to the audience. It is the character's way of testifying to her experience as a political prisoner.

MARIA
Miguel, my compañero, and I were living in Buenos Aires. We thought we were safe.

Two men, dark suits, skinny ties, slicked back hair. A white Falcon at the curb. The tall one asked, "Maria Echevaria?" Why didn't I lie? Say I was the nanny, the housekeeper, a guest -- anything? But no. I nodded. "We'd like a word with you."

MARIA (CONT.)

Francisco must have heard the knock on the door, or heard the fear in my voice, or . . . he began to cry. The taller one, with the perfect white teeth, tilted his head just so, and said, you have a baby?

Again, I should have lied – do we tell, meaningless lies? I said nothing. I didn't need to. Francisco cried again, and my milk let down. Just like that: betrayed by my body.

A woman appeared with another man at my door. The woman never took off her coat and gloves. She simply came up to me and put her hands out for my baby. I held him tighter. She leaned in and whispered, "Just for a few hours 'til they clear things up." *(beat)* They're still trying to clear things up.

My son will be two on the 29th. I have no idea where he is, if he's alive or – I think I'd know if he were – I think I'd feel it, don't you? I think a mother would know.

THE END.

16 "PUCHERO"
from *Compañeras*

Time: Mid-1970s

Place: Punta de Rieles Women's Prison; Montevideo, Uruguay
Guard – mid-20s through 30s.

Up until this point in the play the audience knows very little about the Guard, except she seems to relish carrying out the orders of her commander. She speaks to the audience.

GUARD: I know, you don't want to hear from me. I'm the "bad guy." Well, I have a name, too. It's not Guard, nor Soldier, and no, it's not Dog. I am Caridad Maria Gardel. And I have a family, too. Not married, no kids, but I have a father and – a little brother. My mother died when I was seven, and I've done my best to step into her role cooking, cleaning, and caring for Panchito – that's Carlos, my baby brother. When Mami died, Panchito was barely one. He cried a lot. Colic, they say, but I think he was weeping for our mother. Night after night I walked the floor with him, singing lullabies until my throat grew dry and cracked.
(singing, lullaby)

GUARD (CONT.)
A la puerto del ceilo venden zapatos/ para los angelitos que endan
descalzos
Durmete, nino, duermete nino / Duermete, nino, arru, arru.

As he grew, he began to call me Mami. I never taught him this, I
swear! But out it came. I thought it was sweet, me, now only eight;
he was my little blue-eyed baby.

Then one day my father, still reeling from the death of my mother,
heard Panchito call me Mami, and he slapped him. His hard,
workman's hand left a mark on my brother's cheek. I don't know
what I was thinking, I wasn't thinking, all I felt was rage. I picked up a
piece of wood by the fireplace and smacked my father in the back. I
scooped up Panchito and locked us in the bathroom. Eventually we
had to come out, and he caught up with me and gave me a beating I
will never forget, but even at eight I knew I'd do whatever I had to
protect my baby brother. Whatever it took.

On the night they murdered him, I was preparing his favorite meal,
puchero. It's a simple stew, really, but Panchito always loved it. I was
probably buying the groceries when --
(points to a woman in audience)
– her flyers were circulating in the street, calling people to meet so
that they might plot.

I was probably braising the meat when they gathered at her apartment
in order to decide who would go out on the ambush.
(gestures to another person in audience)
Tossing a salad with lemon juice when that one poured the assassins a
beer.

I was sautéing onions and garlic when her husband's disciples began
to follow my brother down the dark road after he left the police
station for the day.

GUARD (CONT.)
(nods at someone else)
I was setting the table, humming a tango, when her
compañero stopped my brother, a smile on his face, asking
for help with a flat tire. I was putting the warm bread on the
table when he pressed the trigger, sending a bullet into
Panchito's hungry belly. Cold fear crept into my own when
the stew lost its steam. I began to pace the room while she
worked the single bullet out of her companero's leg that my
Panchito got off before they stuck one of their own between
his beautiful blue eyes.

Certainly, the story isn't quite so neat. Maybe these women
had no direct connection to Panchito's death. Maybe it was
somebody else's brother they killed. Ask them, but they'll tell
you they're innocent. Everyone in jail is innocent.
Assassins? Accomplices? This I know: Someone washed
Panchito's blood off their hands that night. But the thing
about blood – it stains. And when I look at them, I see it all
over las compañeras. My name is Caridad Maria Gardel. My
brother was Carlos "Panchito"Gardel. A first year police
officer with blue eyes, black wavy hair, and a dimple in his
chin. I changed his diapers, wiped his tears, taught him to
read. And on Sept. 21st, 1977, I poured dirt on his grave.
(sings)
A los ninos que duermen Dios los bendice/Alas madres que
velan Dios las asiste.
Duermete, nino, duermete, nino,/Duermete, nino, arru, arru.
(beat)
Line up!

THE END.

17 "I TIED HIS SHOES"

from *Compañeras*

Time: Mid-1970s

Place: Punta de Rieles Women's Prison; Montevideo, Uruguay

Teresa - in her late 50s but looks much older. Her back is bent from years of laboring in prison. But there is an obvious dignity to her that rises above all that she has seen and experienced. She has recently been told that she has ovarian cancer and is dying.

TERESA
No, don't feel sorry for me. This is good. For years I have not known how long my sentence is, but now I know – 6 months. Nothing they do can keep me here longer. 6 months. Then I'm free to be with Luis.

There he sat at our kitchen table in his plaid pajamas with a bag over his head and his slippers on his feet as they interrogated him and ransacked our home. -- Oh, Luis was "guilty".

TERESA (CONT.)
With only 6 months left, I think I am free to say this: we
were intent on overthrowing the current dictatorship. And if
they had not imprisoned so many of our leaders, if they had
not disappeared the remaining, or forced them to flee – we
would have accomplished our goal. We may still.

We'd been married for nineteen years, 7 children, ages 5
through 16 when the men came to get him. We were asleep
when we heard the pounding on the door. That's on
purpose, so you're disoriented. It didn't take us long to grasp
the situation, however. We had to open the door, like it or
not. "Are you Luis Bendetti?" As if they didn't know. Luis
said, "I am. What of it?" Immediately, they put the bag over
his head, another man grabbed his arms and tied them
behind his back, forced him into a chair. A third man waved
a gun telling me to sit down at the table. He cut the phone
wires.

They went through every drawer in the house, ripping books
off the shelves, rifling through them before tossing them on
the floor in a heap. After four hours of kicking and hitting a
defenseless man, they turned to me. I looked this thug in the
eyes and I said, "Not a hair on my children's head – not a
single hair on their heads will you touch." I can't believe I
scared them, but they knew with all certainty they would get
nowhere with me.

But then the bastard says, in all but a whisper, "What about
Senor's head?" I knew then. This was it. They were taking
Luis and I would never see him again in this life. Luis was
speaking gently, encouraging me to be strong, telling me he
loved me, but he was speaking through a hood.

TERESA (CONT.)
Then they were taking him. They told me to get his shoes. As I bent down to put my husbands shoes on his feet, I realized this was the last thing I would ever do for him. It was as if I were photographing Luis's feet: There they were. These feet I'd know for 20 years, yet never really examined. They were big feet – size 48, slender and long, with a long second toe, longer than the big one, with fine blond hairs on them. His toe nails needed trimming. Why had I not noticed this before? Why had I not tended to them myself? There was a bunion on the left foot. He had never mentioned it, never complained. I slipped his feet into socks, pulling them up, tenderly around those delicate ankles.

How did those slim ankles ever hold up that tall man? It seemed impossible. Then I helped him slip on his shoes. The black, new wing tips. One man was yelling at me, shouting to hurry. But I took my time as I tied each shoe. Pulling the loops taut, then crossing them, then looping them through, then tight again. Neat ties.

Strong ties, so that he would not have to worry about them coming loose. They never did. Not even when they decapitated him. Those ties held firm. It gives me some small comfort to know my Luis died with his shoes on. The ones I put on him.

THE END.

18 "SCARY TALES"

a monologue

Time: Right now
Place: a girl's bedroom, somewhere.
KELLY – girl, age 11

KELLY
(reading from a thick book of fairy tales)
". . . and they lived happily ever after. " Yeah, sure, like right.
(snaps the book closed)
Until they moved into the castle and she discovered what it
looked like up close: "This joint is falling apart! Ever hear
about screens?
(swats at a fly)
Not to mention windows? And what's with this kitchen?
You don't expect me to cook in a fireplace, do you? In fact,
I hope you don't expect me to cook at all. Do *you* cook?
Oh, like your mother never taught you because you're a
prince? Well, you need to get over that, babe. Like quick.
Cause <u>my</u> daddy? He told me I was <u>his</u> princess and any man
who gets me has to treat <u>me</u> like a Queen. So, unless you
plan on taking out a home equity loan to renovate your
castle, I ain't livin' in this dump."

KELLY (CONT.)

Geez. Like, let's get real. These shouldn't be called "fairy tales," they should be called scary tales! Here's all these girls waiting around to get rescued. Take Rupunzel. She's got this long, long hair. Why does she have to let it down for someone to climb up and rescue her? Why can't she just chop it off herself, tie one end to the bedpost and climb down? Then, when she's like, on the ground, she can yank down the hair and ---- donate it to Locks of Love. I mean, come on, girl, like figure it out!

Then there's Snow White, one of my mom's favorites. But why First, she gets chased into the woods after her stepmother puts out a hit on her. Then, the woodsman tells her he can't kill her because she's <u>so pretty</u> so he tells her to run away. Okay. Fine. Except he kills a deer and cuts out its heart to prove to the evil step-mom that he killed Snow White. Like yuck.

And what about the mirror that started it all? "Who's the fairest of them all?" Nothing sadder than an old beauty queen trying to hold onto her title. Pa-thetic. Anyway, what does Snowy do? She creep into a frat house and goes to sleep in one of the guys' 7 little beds What is she? Stupid? Doesn't she watch TV? Goldie Locks does this too. Doesn't anyone tell these girls it's not only rude to just let yourself in and take a nap in a stranger's bed but <u>dangerous</u>? I mean, knew not to talk to strangers when I was like two, but these girls Hopeless.

Okay, so then the dwarfs come home, and what does Snowy do? Sh decides to stay and, like, clean up after them. I don't care if they ar dwarfs – there are seven – count 'em – seven men!! I have thre brothers and they're pigs! I challenge you: try to teach them to flush Forget about it.

I say, ask for some lumber and build your own house – like that little pig did. On second thought, ask for bricks.

KELLY (CONT.)
So, anyway, we're all supposed to think that Snowy is happy as can be cleaning up after seven little men. "La-dee-da, I love scrubbing out their tighty whities in the river – by hand – on the rocks – because all the birds keep me company!" Right.

Then, what happens? The evil step mom wearing a "disguise"
appears at her door and offers her an apple. Hello? Ever hear about not taking candy from strangers? That goes double for fruit! Razor blades in apples on Halloween, anyone? Please. The girl is hopeless.

And then she dies. Big surprise. The chick has <u>no</u> survival skills. And the freaky little guys love her so much that they refuse to bury her. Ugh. So they put her in a glass coffin where she lies until Prince Charming comes along and kisses her dead, cold lips. I think there's a fancy name for that kind of thing. Necro—something.

Anywaaay. . . Parents, aunts, uncles, do your girls a favor . . . <u>don't</u> read them fairy tales. The girls are lame, the princes are weird and the castles don't have central air or plumbing. Want to give a book?
(holds up a book)
How about a little Suzie Orman? It's never too early to start investing. Now, <u>this</u> -- she'll cherish.

THE END.

19 "COOKIES"
a monologue

Time: Present
Place: Someone's front door.

Sheila (or actor's name) – 10-12 years old, dressed in a Girl Scout uniform - - at least the sash. She's got a clipboard with her.

SHEILA
Beauty? Where did I learn about beauty? Where does every girl learn? From magazines, of course. My big sister has piles of them in her bedroom. She hates for me to mess with her stuff, but whenever she's not around, I sneak into her room. I'd take out the neat pile she keeps by her bed. Carefully, so she wouldn't even know I'd touched them, I'd flip the shiny pages, breathe in the perfume scent, staring at all the faces of the models, memorizing the way they smiled, or didn't, the way they pouted, the way they leaned casually against a car -- or a guy. I studied the way they wore their make-up, the colors of their lipstick and their hair styles. I studied them and I learned. Wanna know what I learned?
I learned they all look alike! They have the same shaped noses, eyes, even the shapes of their heads are the same. They're all the same height, the same weight.

SHEILA (CONT.)
Just like Barbie dolls where they say it's Latina Barbie on the box, but it's really just white Barbie dipped in a color with brown eyes and hair. They change the wigs, duh. That's like the girls in the magazines. They're all the same. Cookie-cutter girls.

After awhile I couldn't tell which magazines I'd looked at and which one's I hadn't. See, they give you this recipe for how to be beautiful: buy this, wear your hair this way, dress that way,
how to make your boyfriend happy – yuck -- but the recipe is like the kind you use with cookie cutters, so every cookie comes out exactly the same. No -- *(looking for word)* -- variety. No surprises. That's what I learned from beauty magazines. And me? I'm nobody's cookie. Not your cupcake, not your honey, not your little pumpkin, sweetie pie. I'm no cookie. But I'll sell you some. How many cases do you want to buy?

THE END.

20 "CATCHING FISH"
from *Trees*

(MARSHA is about 40 years old, no nonsense professional who has just come back from an arduous day of fishing with a woman whe never could stand. She is tired, sunburnt, and furious.)

MARSHA

Oh, you like a good story? Then you'll love this one. We were having a perfectly pleasant time out there, not catching any fish, but still nice and relaxing. Letting the rowboat take us where it wanted, chatting about this and that, when all of a sudden a fishing boat comes by. It practically flips over our little boat with the waves it makes. They couldn't miss us what with Wendy exposing her hooters *for the entire world to see.*

Yeah. She figured no one was around, what was the big deal. But of course there were other boaters. On a day like today? Come on. And she knew it, too. So here comes this boat within ten feet of us, and she jumps up and squeals! Just in case they haven't gotten a good look at her tits. Sorry. I should wash my mouth out.
(She takes a sip of her Scotch.)
Well, I toss her her t-shirt, which she has enough sense to pull on, and this boat pulls over. There are two guys in it, and one of them asks, "How they bitin'?" Instead of telling them to shove off Wendy --

MARSHA (CONT.)

-- proceeds to engage these guys in a discussion about <u>bait.</u>
Finally, after exhausting the topic of leaches or minnows, she
compliments them on the size of their boat. Next thing
they're inviting us to "go for a spin." I suggest that this isn't
such a good idea, sure we're in "you betcha boy" country, but
I saw that movie Fargo, I know what they can do with a
wood chipper. But Wendy?

She must have missed that flick because she hops into their
boat, saying, "Oh, just once around the lake, puh-lease?"
"Fine," I tell her, "just don't leave me out here to row back
to shore by myself." Then she's gone and SIXTY
MINUTES later I'm rowing back to shore – by myself. On
second thought, I'm worried: I hope the fishermen are okay.

THE END.

Ten-Minute Plays

(Most of the plays have all female casts, but there are a few which include a bit part for a man.)

21 "MOURNING COFFEE"
DRAMA/COMEDY

Time: Present, morning.

Place: kitchen of low-income home. Required on stage are a small refrigerator, a Mr. Coffee, a counter top to rest the coffee maker on, which should include a drawer for utensils, and a table for two with chairs. Off-stage left is the bathroom, and off-stage right is the entrance.

Adele Jamison - a woman in her late 60s on up. She is feisty, and probably somewhat difficult to live with. Her life is one long routine; she follows the same path through her home day after day, even when the routine is no longer applicable to her life.

Paramedic - male or female, age can be anywhere from 22 on up. Ordinary individual who steps into Adele's world ever so briefly at the end of the play.

Note: There are three endings to this short play. All should be performed, as they are not optional endings but takes on the play's resolution.

Ending "A" provides the predictable response, Ending "B" provides a somewhat ironic response, and Ending "C" should come as a bit of a surprise. Perhaps the character experiences each ending on different mornings, sampling alternative approaches to the same situation.

(Adele enters from s.r. in a housedress and slippers. She shuffles into the kitchen and goes about the morning's preparations. It's a ritual she's been doing for decades. First she goes to the refrigerator where she gets a pitcher of cold water. She then goes to the Mr. Coffee and pours the water into the coffee carafe, then pours the carafe into the coffee maker. Next, she finds a coffee filter and places it in the machine. She removes the plastic lid from the can of coffee, takes the scoop from within in it, and mutters disgustedly.)

ADELE
There's barely a tablespoon here, Willy! Couldn't use this up last time, could you? No, let Adele open another can.

(She dumps the last of the grains into the filter, stoops down and retrieves a new can from the cabinet below the coffee maker. She searches through a utensil drawer for the hand can opener.)

Now, where did you put the opener? It goes at the front of the drawer. The <u>front.</u>

(At last she finds it and begins to struggle with the can opener, which seems to bite into the metal and work for a few turns, then gets stuck. Over and over she turns and removes it, turns and removes it, muttering all the while under her breath.)

Would it kill you to buy me an electric can opener? What do they cost at Ace Hardware, huh? Ten bucks? Eleven bucks? But what do you know about electric can openers? You never opened a god damned can in your life.

ADELE (CONT.)
(Finally, she gets the metal top to give and removes the circle.)

Hallelujah and praise the coffee!

(She ends up cutting her finger.)

Damn! I just want a stinking cup of coffee.

(She goes searching through the drawer again for a bandage, finally finds one and goes through the machinations of putting it on her wounded finger.)

One day, just one day, it'd be nice if you would get up before me and make the coffee. Is that asking too much, ay Willy?

(She continues the process of putting grains into the filter, finally finishing and turning on the machine. Coffee soon begins to brew as she moves on to the next step: getting the cups and saucers, placing these on the small table for two, getting the milk out, pouring this into a pitcher, finding a couple of spoons, and bringing these to the table.)

We been married how many -- 47? Forty-seven years and you never made the morning coffee. Forty-seven years you jump out of bed, grab the newspaper, and disappear into the bathroom. And you never get off the commode 'til you're done with the sports section. Just in time for a fresh, hot cup of coffee ready to be poured. Well, ain't that just grand?

(Next she goes to the breadbasket and removes four slices of bread and puts these in the toaster. She returns the pitcher of water to the fridge and searches for something.)

Willy? Willy, did you use the last of the margarine? Where did he put it?

ADELE (CONT.)
(She peers into the refrigerator, moves things around, searching.
They make this little door, and that's where the margarine
goes. Right inside the little door. Not on the shelf, not in
the freezer, behind the little door. Well, I can't find it. We
must be out. Let's see . . . we've got . . . grape, a spoonful
left, and . . . orange. Blah! Where did this come from? Two
Christmases ago? Lou-Ann and that Family Farmer sampler
pack?

Well, that's it. It's either a drop of grape or you got orange.
Willy? Ain't you done in there yet?

*(Adele puts the jelly jars on the table, gets a butter knife out of the
drawer. Everything is set. The coffee is done (or done enough) and she
pours the steaming liquid into the cups. About now the toast pops up
and she places this on a plate and brings it to the table. Everything is
set. She sits, fixes her coffee, takes the first sip, enjoying it. She pauses.
Listening.)*

Willy? The toast is getting cold. If you don't get out here
now you're gonna get stuck with the orange marmalade.

*With a sigh, she gets up and goes to the bathroom door o.s. She raps on
it.*
Did you go back to sleep in there?
(Knocks again)
Willy? Will –?

*(Momentarily, she backs up into view, trembling. She looks around,
spots the telephone, and grabs it, dialing.)*

Yes! My husband, I think he's – he may have had a heart
attack. Yes! He's unconscious or – 4581 Belmont Road.

ADELE (CONT.)
That's right. Adele – Adele Jamison. Okay, okay, thank you.

She returns the phone to its cradle, goes and sits at the table, pours milk in each cup, then sugar in what would be Willy's, puts orange jam on one piece of toast this she gives herself. Puts grape jam on another piece of toast, this she places on Willy's plate. She sips at her coffee, tears streaming down her face. She waits.

LIGHTS

The additional endings are just that, not alternatives but scenes which should be performed in addition.

Ending "B"

(When the lights come back up, Adele is holding the phone.)

ADELE
Yes! My husband, I think he's – he may have had a heart attack. Yes He's unconscious or – 4581 Belmont Road. That's right. Adele – Adele Jamison. Okay, okay, thank you.

(She returns the phone to its cradle, then goes and sits at the table, methodically fixing her cup of coffee, then reaching first for the orange marmalade, then think better and takes the grape, scraping the last of it off the sides and spreading it on her toast. She has her breakfast, looking content.)

LIGHTS

"Ending C"

(When the lights come back up, Adele is holding the phone.)

ADELE (CONT.)
Yes! My husband, I think he's – he may have had a heart attack. Yes! He's unconscious or – 4581 Belmont Road. That's right. Adele – Adele Jamison. Okay, okay, thank you.

(She returns the phone to its cradle. Goes and sits at the table. Fixes her coffee, fixes her toast, and proceeds to eat. There is a RAP at the door. Adele does not move, but continues to sip her coffee. Fierce RAPPING is heard.)

PARAMEDIC (o.s.)
Mrs. Jamison? This is the Grand Forks' Rescue Squad.

ADELE
Come in!

(The sound of a door opening. A paramedic rushes in.)

PARAMEDIC
Ma'am? You called? Your husband – ma'am?

(Adele gestures with her head toward the bathroom. Paramedic goes in the direction she's gestured to, and disappears o.s. Adele gets up and gets the pot of coffee. The paramedic returns, looking puzzled.)

PARAMEDIC
Ma'am? There's no one in there.

ADELE
How do you feel about orange marmalade?

PARAMEDIC
But you called – you thought your husband –

ADELE
Willy? He's been dead for years. How do you take your morning coffee, dear?

THE END.

22 "A COUPLE OF BOOBS"
Drama/Comedy, mild sexual references

Time: Present

Place: Exam room at a hospital

Mother - mid-50s, up beat despite circumstances

Daughter - mid-20s, terrified

The two women do not look at each other. They look anywhere but at each other until the very last lines of the play. The mother is in a hospital gown. The daughter is in street clothes.

MOTHER
I woke up one morning and then they were there. Like two ripe peaches.

DAUGHTER
I kept wishing they'd grow. Every night, before I went to bed and after I brushed my teeth, I would do those exercises, you know -- "I must, I must, I must increase my bust –

MOTHER
(Joins in)
"The better, the better to fit into my sweater." Johnny Nelson who was two years older than me but in the same grade told me that if I let him massage them, it would help them grow.

DAUGHTER
Pig! *(Pause)*

DAUGHTER
Mother! You didn't?

MOTHER
Every girl in my class was quickly filling their B-cups. Why, Joanna Gilstad was overflowing in a C! My girls were so pathetically behind, I had to do something.

DAUGHTER
But –

MOTHER
So one day, after school, we climbed up into my tree house and I lifted my shirt up –

DAUGHTER
How old were you?!

MOTHER
Why, thirteen or so.

DAUGHTER
Thirteen! You wouldn't even let me ride my bike to the park at 13!

MOTHER
Of course not. So there we were in the tree house my father had built never imagining the use I'd put it to. There on the gritty floor, the smell of pine thick in the warm air, big clumsy Johnny, oh, so tenderly cupped my budding breasts.

DAUGHTER
Copping a feel, you mean.

MOTHER
No, cupping my breasts. The look on his face when he saw them – my! It was like he was gazing upon the Holy Grail – grails.

DAUGHTER
They were his first boobs, outside of Playboy, I'm sure. Pig.

MOTHER
He was so delicate, and he had these big meaty paws, I mean, when he played baseball he didn't need a mitt. Big paws. Calloused from working in the fields, but smooth, like a river stone. His hand swallowed my tender breasts whole. I could feel the heat from his palms and they seared me, but I feel myself arch up, up into those palms.

DAUGHTER
Does Daddy know about this?

MOTHER
Then he took his index finger, as thick as a sausage, and gentle, ever so gentle circled the areola, then the nipples, and it felt – exquisite. My eyes were closed but I could feel him staring at me, at them, I heard his breathing – or rather, lack of as he held his breath for long minutes. And when I opened my eyes I saw that his were wide and wet. And –

DAUGHTER
Look, maybe I don't need to —

MOTHER
— he said, in this low, husky voice filled with, with something, wha would you call it?

DAUGHTER
Let's see -- lust?

MOTHER
No, no, it wasn't like that, the look on his face, it was — appreciation Gratitude. And just like that he carefully pulled my shirt over m girls. And I asked, is that it? Do you think they'll grow now? And h said, "You have nothing to worry about. They're -- perfect just th way they are."
(Long pause)

DAUGHTER
Mama — they're not <u>you.</u> You're more than a couple of boobs.

MOTHER
I know. It's just hard to say good-bye. You should have seen them a 20! Whew! Before gravity took over? And at 25, on our honeymoon your father and I got naked in Cancun.

DAUGHTER
I don't believe it! Daddy?

MOTHER
Prancing in the waves in his birthday suit. White porcelain butt an all. It felt so wonderful to swim in the sea, the water lapping on m breasts, the sun kissing them.

DAUGHTER
I can't picture this. (Pause) On second thought, I can. Let's move on.

MOTHER
Well, there was this two-piece red bathing suit, boy could I turn heads back then. How do you suppose <u>you</u> came along? My ass was okay, my legs? Nothing to brag about. But these girls? These girls caught you father's fancy and boom, next thing I know you're at my breast. Then your brother, and his brother. 3 babies in a row, why I felt like I'd never get the girls back to myself. But, eventually, I did. And they were a little worse for the wear, I will admit, but I just scooped 'em up and filled them into some expensive bras. Pink satin, black lace, front closures, under-wires, I had a fetish for bras. I looked forward to JC Penny's bra sales – two for one. I was a feminist but there was no way I would have burned a bra in the '70s. In fact, I think that's just a bunch of propaganda, anyway. For Pete's sake, what woman in her right mind would burn a 30-dollar bra! It'd be a sin, that's what it'd be. (*Pause*) I guess I won't need them. The bras.

DAUGHTER
You'll have reconstructive surgery. You'll see. We'll go to Penny's. You'll see.

MOTHER
There just a couple of boobs, I don't know why . . .

(*Daughter finally turns to her mother, and turns her to face her*)

MOTHER
They were perfect.

DAUGHTER
You're perfect just the way you are. Alive.

MOTHER
Do you think — No.

DAUGHTER
What?

MOTHER
Never mind. It was stupid.

DAUGHTER
Look, you told me about Johnny groping you and Dad's porcelain ass skinny-dipping; I think you can tell me something stupid. Say.

MOTHER
Remember cousin, Jeannie? After she had her gallstones removed, she asked for them, and she has them in a little baby food jar in her linen closet. I was –

DAUGHTER
Mother!

MOTHER
You know, it seems some wrong that a mother should continually shock her daughter. Dear, you need to let loose a bit more.

DAUGHTER
You're joking, though, I mean, Mom, that's so – morbid.

MOTHER
What? To ask the surgeon for my breasts after he – Why? What's he going to do with them, toss them in the garbage – *human waste*?

DAUGHTER
But, you can't —

MOTHER
They're mine, I can do anything I damn well please with them. From letting some boy touch them who'd die three years later in Vietnam to letting them float free in the Gulf of Mexico! They're mine. Mine.

DAUGHTER
But — what — ?

MOTHER
What would I do with them? Don't worry; I wouldn't keep them in a jar next to the towels. No, I think, I think what I'd like to do is bury them. In a pink satin box on my father's land. Oh, the tree house is long gone, but the pine tree, it might still be there. I'd dig deep into the moist soil and lay the box down. The place where they began to blossom.
(Long pause)

DAUGHTER
Mother — I'd go with —

MOTHER
Silly idea. Anyway, they're just a couple of boobs. But, oh, they were beautiful.

THE END.

23 "Something Borrowed, Someone Blue"
Comedy, Strong Language

Time: Present

Place: Private room in a church in New Jersey

Loraine – the 20-something bride

Felicia – the 20-something maid of honor

Loraine is wearing a wedding dress, standing in front of a full-length mirror, primping. Her best friend, FELICIA, dressed in a frou-frou bride's maid dress, is fluffing her veil in the back. FELICIA looks less than enthusiastic.

LORAINE
So?

FELICIA
You make a beautiful bride, Loraine.

LORAINE
And?

FELICIA
(Sadly)
And, and, I'm sure you'll both be very happy?

LORAINE
And?

FELICIA
And, and, and – I wish your mother could be here, God rest her soul.

LORAINE
And? Felicia– I told you not to forget anything. As my maid of honor it's your responsibility not to forget anything.

FELICIA
Oh! The ring! Right here!
(She pulls a gold band out of her bra)

LORAINE
Not Felix's ring! And can't you keep my husband's ring somewhere else, for Christ's sake?

FELICIA
Husband-to-be. He's not your husband yet. Just the groom. Besides I won't have my purse, and this dress doesn't have pockets.

LORAINE
Oh, stop your yabbering! I wasn't talking about the ring, anyway. There's a little superstition you seem to have forgotten, and I'm not getting married unless we include it.

FELICIA
What? Oh! I almost forgot!
(She takes a penny out of her bra and holds it up)
A copper penny for your shoe.

LORAINE
What else do you keep in that Playtex of yours?
(Grabs the penny and removes her shoe, placing it in it)
But that wasn't what I was thinking. Come on now, I picked you for
    maid of honor over my sister. Don't let me down, girl.

FELICIA
I don't know what you're talking about. I didn't let the groom see his
bride, I bought the rice, you've got the white dress, even though we
both know you've been doing it -

(Knock on door)

Dean (o.s.)
Five minutes, Ladies! Everything okay?

LORAINE
Just swell! We'll be right there, Dean!

Dean (o.s)
No cold feet, you hear?

LORAINE
Not this bride!

Dean (o.s.)
That's a relief!

LORAINE
Now, where the hell is it? Something old, something new, something borrowed, something blue!

FELICIA
It totally slipped my mind. Guess you can't get married.

LORAINE
Don't be a fool. Let's start with the old.
(Sticks out her hand)
Give me your necklace.

FELICIA
(Puts a hand to her necklace)
My dead grandmother gave me this on my 13th birthday.
LORAINE
Perfect, it's old and it's blue! We can kill two birds. Hand it over.

FELICIA
But, but my grandmother's dead, and I loved her, and –

LORAINE
I paid for your liposuction.

(FELICIA grudgingly removes the necklace and hands it over.)

FELICIA
Couldn't we call it borrowed? Then you could give it back after the ceremony.

LORAINE
We'd be pushing it if we called it borrowed, too. So, how about new?

FELICIA
You're taking my grandmother's necklace, isn't that new enough?

LORAINE
No, it's not. Look, do you want to jinx my marriage? It says something old, something new, something borrowed, something blue. Where's my new?

FELICIA
But I forgot to get you something. Maybe you should call off the wedding. I'll tell Felix if you don't want to face him.

LORAINE
As if! Do you know what I had to pay the priest to marry us? Not to mention the reception hall? I'd never get my deposit back. Just, just look in your purse. Maybe you have some gum or something.
(LORAINE dumps the contents of her purse onto the chair.)

FELICIA
This is ridiculous. I don't chew gum. You'll just have to get married without anything new. Take the chance. It's just a stupid superstition.

LORAINE
It may be stupid, but I'm not risking it. You know how I feel about superstitions. Ever since I was a kid and I broke my leg on Friday the 13th, I've done my best to be cautious when it comes to them. Spill some salt, throw a pinch over my left shoulder. See a black cat coming, cross the street. Some people think it's silly, but my Aunt Aggie, she broke a mirror and it was nothing but bad luck for 7 years. My cousin Joey stole that car, ended up in Juvie, her husband cheated on her with that bitch from the dry cleaners, and she had nothing but hemorrhoids for 7 years -- my aunt not the bitch, unfortunately. When the 7 years were up, they miraculously cleared up. The doctor said he'd never seen anything like it before. So? Where's my something new?

FELICIA
Okay, hold out your hand.
(She puts a roll of peppermints in her hand)

LORAINE
Oh, Leesh, Lifesavers, you shouldn't have. Really, you put too much thought into it.

FELICIA
It barely suffices as something new. I think you're right. It's an omen. You shouldn't' get married.

LORAINE
Stop saying that. Look, not even opened. They'll due. Of course, how you forget something that's a tradition like this beats the hell out of me. You aren't trying to sabotage me are you?

FELICIA
Of course not! Why would you think that? We've been best friends since 5th grade at St. Joe's. It's just -- you, you-- told me to do so many things: order the food, dye the shoes, see to the flowers, arrange your shower AND your bachelorette party –

LORAINE
Oh, yeah, you screwed that one up, too. I wanted a stripper dressed as a hot cop! You got me a gay, tap dancing telegram!

FELICIA
He was cute. He had dimples.

LORAINE
I wanted to see dimples on a hunk's butt not on the face of a musical theatre major from Montclair State! You know, you've been acting stranger and stranger the closer we've gotten to my wedding day. What is it? Are you afraid you're going to lose me? Why, look! You're about to cry! Aw, that's so sweet. Come here.
(Grabs Felicia in a hug)
You're closer to me than my real sister -- that drunk. And when Felix and I have our first baby, you'll be the godmother!

FELICIA
Loraine -- Loraine, there's something I've got to tell you.

(Knock on door)

Dean (o.s.)
Loraine, your groom is getting nervous. Can we start the wedding march?

FELICIA
Can we get one more minute? Huh? One more fucking minute, ay Dean?

Dean
Uh, yeah, sure! *(Feet running away)*

LORAINE
Felicia?

FELICIA
You cannot marry Felix.

LORAINE
You don't think he's good enough for me? Aw –
(Goes to hug her again, but FELICIA turns her back)

FELICIA
Believe me, it's not that.
(She turns away from her and removes something from her bodice and looks at it.)

LORAINE
What then? What? Are you crying? What do you have to cry about? It's not your wedding day.
(LORAINE spins her around)

FELICIA (crying)
I know!

LORAINE
What's that you're holding? Is that – a picture?
(Grabs for it, but FELICIA pulls it away)
Who is that? Is that –

(She makes a lunge for it but again Loraine manages to snatch it away. This time it tears in half.)

FELICIA
Now, look what you did!

LORAINE
(Looks at the half a photo in her hand)
Whose arm is that around your shoulder?
(Gets it)
I know that hand on your breast! That's Felix's hand! What's my Felix doing grabbing your tit!

(FELICIA is feverishly kissing the remainder of the photo.)

FELICIA
I'm sorry, Loraine, I couldn't help myself! Those dreamy eyes, those broad shoulders, the way he slurps his beer. It's so sexy.

LORAINE
But he's mine!
(She lunges for the other half of the photo)

FELICIA
You're wrong, Loraine! I met him first! Remember? I introduced him to you down the shore.

LORAINE
But you weren't dating him!

FELICIA
I didn't get a chance! The night I introduced him to you -- you slept with him!

LORAINE
That's a lie!

FELICIA
You got him drunk, you drove him home, and you seduced my man, Loraine!

LORAINE
He wasn't your man!

FELICIA
You never gave me a chance!

LORAINE
(Waving picture in air)
Apparently you took your chance!

FELICIA
Give me that! After today, it's all I have left of the sweet memory of the man you stole from me!

LORAINE
I'm going to ask this once, and I want a straight answer: Felicia, have you been sleeping with Felix?

FELICIA
Not until last night.

LORAINE
And then?

FELICIA
We fucked like rabbits 'til dawn.

LORAINE
Must you be so crude?

FELICIA
Why sugar coat it? The truth is out. Now, you can't marry
him. You won't.

LORAINE
You'd like that, wouldn't you?
(Loraine goes and opens the door.)
There are 600 people out there waiting for me to walk down
the aisle and marry Felix. Do you have any idea how much
this frickin' wedding is costing me?

FELICIA
(Closing the door)
But you can't, he's been unfaithful!

LORAINE
One night.

FELICIA
Over and over, all night.

LORAINE
Because you tempted him. You went to his room.

FELICIA
He opened the door.

LORAINE
You flashed your tits.

FELICIA
He grabbed them.

LORAINE
He couldn't help himself. He rationalized, "one last fling.
Never again." He'd be faithful from this day forward.

FELICIA
But the night before your wedding!

LORAINE
Bad timing. True. But, what do you expect me to do? This is a designer gown!

FELICIA
You could save it for when the right guy comes along.

LORAINE
It'd be jinxed. Bad luck. And anyway, Felix is the right guy. He slipped, made a mistake. Besides, did I tell you I opened some of the wedding presents? We got Waterford!

FELICIA
You won't do it! He's a bum, a scoundrel; you won't marry him today!

LORAINE
Don't I look like a woman about to get married?
(She peels open the Lifesavers)
You were a last minute fling. Nothin' more.
(Pops a Lifesaver in her mouth)
Felix loves me.
(Hands the rest to FELICIA)

FELICIA
But, but he cheated with your best friend the night before your wedding day!

LORAINE
That's right, this is MY wedding day.
(Opens door)
Oh, look! Is Felix waiting at the altar for you?
No, that'd be for me.
     (Felicia waves and blows a kiss)

FELICIA
Why, look at the rock on my finger. That's five carats, toots. Count'em. Let's see? *(Grabbing her hand)*
Nope, no diamond on your finger.

FELICIA
I have his seed in my womb!

LORAINE
You slut! *(Slaps her)*
Now move before you make me strangle you with my veil.
(She smoothes out her veil)

FELICIA
But, but you're missing something! Remember? Something old, something new, something borrowed, something blue? Ha! You haven't borrowed anything!

LORAINE
(Takes a look a the torn photo still in her hand, holds it up)
I think I'll borrow Felix, but don't count on me giving him back any time soon.
(She stuffs the rest of the picture into FELICIA's bodice and flounces off stage.)

FELICIA
That doesn't count! You'll see. You'll divorce in a year! Less than that! And he'll come back to me. I'll be waiting. Mark my words! I'll be wating!
(We hear the tune for "Here Comes the Bride.")

THE END.

24 "The Hole Story"
comedy

Time: Christmas Holidays

Place: An icehouse on a lake in North Dakota or Minnesota

The ice house can be nicely outfitted or minimally, but there must be two seats, an already drilled fishing hole, some rods, a small ice bucket, and small kerosene heater. Perhaps there's also a touch of the Christmas spirit in here: a string of lights or a tiny tree. The playwright suggests conveying a small space by pulling stage curtains in, leaving about a six-foot gap. The fact that this is a narrow space plays out in the story and adds to the humor.

GLADYS - mid-50s thru 60s woman with a playful sense of humor. She likes a little "nip" now and then, and because of the stress of a house full of family the "now" is right now.

GLORIA - about the same age, the slightly older sister, her sense of humor is dryer, and she's dying for a cigarette.

(GLORIA enters the "Ice House" and turns on the gas heater. She proceeds to open the fish hole.)

GLORIA
Anybody home?

She reaches for her rod and reel and sinks the line in the hole without baiting it. Then she looks around, rubbing her mittened hands together.

(GLADYS enters.)

GLADYS
Hey.

GLORIA
Hey. Did you get them?

(GLADYS nods.)

GLADYS
You?

GLORIA
You betcha. Now hand 'em over.

GLADYS
Hold your horses. Let me get my rod out.

GLORIA
Forget that shit. Hand 'em over.

(GLADYS purposely takes her time getting her rod, sinking the line in the hole. Then she reaches in her coat and pulls out a pack of cigarettes. GLORIA grabs them.)

GLADYS
Those things will kill you.

GLORIA
So I hear. Well?

GLADYS
Well?

GLORIA
Lighter? Matches? Tell me you didn't forget.

GLADYS
You didn't say anything about those. You simply said, "Steal me some smokes."

GLORIA
Gladys, it's a given. What, am I suppose to rub two sticks together?

GLADYS
You've always been the resourceful type. Heck, you built this place. I'm sure you could create fire from sticks.

GLORIA
Tell me your shittin' me.

GLADYS *(pulls out a lighter and flicks it)*
I'm shittin' you.

GLORIA
(Grabs for the lighter and it goes into the hole)
Aw, crap!

GLADYS
Uh, oh! Maybe I could –

GLORIA squats down, pushing her coat sleeve up, and reaches her hand into the hole.

GLORIA
I think I – I - I –
(She backs up, her arm dripping)

GLADYS
Did you get it?

(GLORIA glares at her, shaking the water off her arm.)

GLADYS
I could go back to the house, and –

GLORIA
Yeah, and then they'll be looking for their pie and coffee. Forget it.
(GLORIA finds a towel and dries off her arm)

GLADYS
I was just trying to have a little fun with you, and I didn't --

GLORIA
Forget it.
(She picks up her rod and jiggles it around.)

GLADYS
I really didn't mean –

GLORIA
I said, "Forget it."

(Beat.)

GLADYS
Did you bring mine?

GLORIA
I did.

GLADYS
Could I -- have it?

GLORIA
'suppose.

(GLORIA reaches into her coat pocket and brings out a pint-size bottle of Jack Daniels. She hands it to her, but drops it in the hole just as GLADYS is about to grab it. GLADYS makes a save, though.)

GLADYS
Ha!
(She twists off the cap and takes a long sip.)
I can't believe you'd be so spiteful. It was an accident.

GLORIA
Uh-huh.

GLADYS
We're sisters! I wouldn't do something like that to you.

GLORIA
Of course you would, we're sisters. Plus, you hate it when I smoke.

GLADYS
I don't care if you smoke! I'm not one of those.

GLORIA
Correction, you hate it when I smoke in here.

GLADYS
Well, it is a small space.

GLORIA
So you did do it on purpose.

GLADYS
I swear I didn't. Look, give me one of those cancer sticks.

GLORIA
No.

GLADYS
I said, "Give me one."

GLORIA
I'll smoke them later. All of them. In one sitting. Quickly.
Suck 'em down one after the other. *(Makes sucking noises)*

GLADYS
I'll light it for you.

GLORIA
How?

GLADYS
Just give me one! Hurry, they'll be looking for us a soon as they realize they haven't eaten in an hour.

(GLORIA hands over a cigarette, cautiously.)

(GLADYS gets down on her knees in front of the heater, putting the cigarette in her mouth.)

GLORIA
Uh, Gladys, look it's okay. I believe you, all right? Gladys?

GLADYS
Do you want to have a smoke or not?

GLADYS holds her face and the cigarette close to the heater, the cigarette finally gets lit, and she hands it over with a flourish.

GLADYS (cont.)
Ta-da!

GLORIA
Ah!
(GLORIA points to GLADYS's hair.)

GLADYS
What?

(GLORIA smacks at GLADYS's head repeatedly.)

GLADYS
Ow! Ow! What?! What are you doing?!

GLORIA
Your hair's on fire!

(GLORIA finds a small ice bucket, and reaches into the hole and hauls up some water, throwing it at GLADYS's head)

GLADYS
Why the hell'd you do that!?
(Grabs for the towel)

GLORIA
You were on fire. Was I supposed to let you burn?

(GLADYS examines her hair, which is now partially wet, along with the front of her parka. She removes this and hangs it on a hook.

GLADYS
(Sitting down, examining hair)
It doesn't look singed.

GLORIA
I saved it in time. My, this is good. Who'd you steal them from?

GLADYS
Vern. He comes up to watch the game. Took 'em right out of his coat pocket.

GLORIA
Nice work.

GLADYS
(Takes a sip off the bottle)
This?

GLORIA
Ben keeps it in the car in case the truck breaks down in a storm.

GLADYS
Remind me to get stuck with that boy and not my husband. Ralph just has a couple of old nuts and some hard candy.

GLORIA
I bet he does.

GLADYS whacks her.
Then they settle into their chairs and sit in silence enjoying their particular vices for a beat or two.

GLADYS
You got some bait on that line?

GLORIA
Nah.

GLADYS
Why'd you even put it in the hole?

GLORIA
It's an icehouse. It's a fishing rod. But bait? Too much trouble.

GLADYS
Kinda cozy out here.

GLORIA
Listen. Can you hear it?
(Beat)
That's called "quiet." No darling daughters who won't let you smoke in your own house.

GLADYS
No husbands hollering for a this or a that and won't get off their asse

GLORIA
No precious grandbabies.

GLADYS
They are precious.

GLORIA
But it's been a week.

GLADYS
I know. But they are precious.

GLORIA
There's a saying . . . fish and relatives in the house -- both start to stink after a week.

GLADYS
True, you're lucky, though. At least it isn't your son-in-law who ends every speech with a good old scratch of his balls.

GLADYS
He does not!

GLORIA
Notice. Blah, blah, blah.
(She scratches at her crotch)

(GLADYS and GLORIA break into rocking laughter until finally they're wiping at their eyes.)

GLORIA (cont.)
Ah, well, it's quiet out here.

(They sit and appreciate the silence.)

GLADYS
How you suppose Mama stood it all those years? Two daughters, three sons, all of us married, at least for a while, grand kids tearing up her place.

GLORIA
Papa.

GLADYS
Papa. *(Pause)* I don't think she ever ducked into an icehouse. Where'd she go when she couldn't take one more minute of us?

GLORIA
It wasn't an icehouse, but she did have a hideout. And when the goin' got rough, she'd sneak away and steal a smoke, too.

GLADYS
Where?

GLORIA
The root cellar. Ever notice how she just had to see if there was enough canned rhubarb? Or maybe it was green beans. Could a been beets. Didn't matter. What mattered was it was dark and quiet down there.

GLADYS
Ha. So even Mama had a hideout. I always thought she was a saint, and I'd never be that patient.

GLORIA
I got a feeling that the less saintly she felt, the more she needed to check those canned beets. Right behind them, pushed back out of sight was a jar lid she used as an ashtray, and that's where she kept her smokes.

GLADYS
Mama?

GLORIA
Mama.

GLADYS
Who'd a thunk.
(Long beat)
Maybe we should use some bait.

GLORIA
Yeah, but if we catch something ...

GLADYS
We'd have to clean it.

GLORIA
Exactly.

GLADYS
Then they'd expect us to fry it.

GLORIA
Uh-huh.

GLADYS
Better this way.

GLORIA
That's my thought.

GLADYS
I didn't drop it --

GLORIA
I know. Your hair wasn't on fire, either.
(She finishes her cigarette, and tosses it in the hole.)

GLADYS
You mean – ?
(GLORIA nods, gives a little giggle)
I got water in my ear! My bra is soaked! I'll get you for this.

GLORIA
You can try. Well?
(She tosses the last of her cigarette into the hole then stands.)
Shall we return to playing hostess?

GLADYS
Hold on a sec.
(She pulls out a candy cane and peels it back, sucking on it)
Breath.   Wouldn't want to ruin my sainted image, doncha know.

(GLORIA pulls out the rods, leans them against the wall, then closes the hole.)

GLORIA
See you later, ladies.

GLADYS
We'll be back.

GLORIA
Oh, you betcha.

(They exit.)

THE END.

25 "Lenora the Disco Queen"
from The Nut Lab

Comedy

This is a scene from the play that can either be played as a stand-alone scene or excerpted for Lenora's monologue.

Time: Present

Place: Human Nutrition Lab, dormitory for subjects undergoing observation – women's room

Lenora – a fiftyish woman who is often weepy, and always nervous.

Jenny – early-twenties, fairly normal with one minor exception – her ever present sock puppet that she sometimes uses to speak for her.

Walleye – non-speaking role in this scene, he's an aging hippy

(The women are seated on their individual beds).

JENNY
You said you've lost a sense of who you are since you became Harry's wife. Well? Who were you before you got married? *(Using the sock puppet)* Were you always so wimpy?

LENORA
Wimpy? You think I'm wimpy? Well, maybe I am. No. I wasn't always this way.

JENNY
Well, then, how were you?

LENORA
I was a dancer!

JENNY
You mean like ballet?

LENORA
No, no, no. Like disco. Oh, you should have seen me at 18, Jenny! I had all the moves.

(She does a few of her "moves." The lights dim and a disco ball materializes, and Lenora steps into a spot. Walleye steps forward to oblige in a dance.)

LENORA
I was a Dancing Queen, twirling from man to man, my feet a blur on the linoleum of the VFW. I loved putting on my heels, the way they showed off my calves, how I'd raise one in an elegant dip, the polyester of my skirt sliding down the length of my nylon panty hose until the material pooled at my cha-cha oh, so briefly, causing the men's jaws to drop. Then my partner's strong arms would pull me upright, and we'd continue the push pull, our bodies throbbing to the disco beat. "Love to love you, baby! Oo, love to love you baby!"

Oh, the feel of a man's arms who could take the lead, moving me around the dance floor, pulling my body into his, my girls pressing against his chest, the scent of sweat and Halston and sex all stewing together. And if he were a stranger? All the more exciting as his hands glanced off my waist, brushing my ample bumpty "accidentally." Sometimes, no often, when he held me tight I could feel his smoking kielbasa pressing –

LENORA (CONT.)
--against my cha-cha.

I was a regular fixture, Friday, Saturday night, you'd find me down at the VFW or the K of C spinning, and dipping, and shaking my thang! I danced all night; one fella after another would ask me. I never sat down. And all week long I dreamed of the weekend while I worked at the paint store.

JENNY
A paint store? Isn't that just like –

LENORA
I was staying alive! UH-UH-UH- UH --

JENNY
So, why did you -- sit down?

LENORA
I met Harry.

(Walleye kisses her hand, spotlight goes out and Lenora returns to the reality of the room.)

LENORA
He showed up at the VFW one night. I can still see him standing there in his baby blue leisure suit, his gold St. Christopher medal catching the light of the disco ball. He leaned against the bar as I twirled around the dance floor. His eyes only on me. When the music ended, I was full of confidence. I strutted over to him and said, "Hey, mister, want to dance?"

JENNY
Wow! You weren't afraid to ask a boy to dance?

LENORA
I was Lenora the Disco Queen; no one turned me down. Until Harry.

JENNY
He said no!?

LENORA
He didn't know how to disco. Had two left feet. But he had this dimple in his chin: a tiny hiney. So, I sat the next dance out. I been sitting out the next dance ever since.

JENNY
But you must have missed it! Dancing was such a big part of you.

LENORA
Oh, Harry took me out -- bowling or to the stock car races. Sometimes we'd go to classic car shows. Harry loves classic car shows.

JENNY
What about you?

LENORA
Eh. You seen one 1966 Mustang in prime you seen 'em all.

JENNY
Well, I think you should do something about this.

LENORA
There's nothing to do. Donna Summers became a born again Christian and three of the Bee Gees are gone. Gloria Gaynor might be surviving somewhere, but she was a one-hit wonder.

JENNY
Maybe you could try something new – salsa or – or take a Zumba class!

LENORA

You don't get it, do you? You with your college books and your dreams of being a psychologist! You're young, single, your wings haven't been clipped. How can you possibly understand?

(Goes to door)

Let me spell it out for you, honey: I'm too old, I'm too fat, and disco is dead!

(Slams out of room as the first notes of "Staying Alive" start to play)

THE END.

25 "Calabozo"
from *Compañeras*
drama – strong language

While this scene includes others, it could easily be cut to work a a powerful monologue.

Time: late 1970s

Place: Punta de Rieles women's prison, Montevideo, Uruguay – specifically the calobozo – solitary confinement.

Characters:

Women – off-stage sing, and later knocking

Ana – Mid-20s to mid-30s. A true political revolutionary. Tough, cynical, but not without a tender side.

Guard – woman about the same age as Ana. Cold.

Lights down. From the dark come women's voices singing a folk song:

WOMAN (O.S.)
Arroz con leche/ Me quiero casar

ANOTHER WOMAN (O.S.)
(Joins in singing, getting louder)
Con una senorita/ que sepa bordar
con esta si/ con esta no / con esta senorita, me caso you!

(A square of light comes up on a corner of the stage, the sound of a cell door opens with a squeal of iron. A mattress is tossed onto the floor, then Ana is pushed into the light by Guard.)

ANA
There's no bunk for my mattress.

GUARD
It's the calabozo. You were looking for a five star hotel? Get in there.

ANA
How long?

GUARD
As long as the Captain decides.

ANA
Can't you tell me? So I can –

GUARD
Get in the cell.

ANA
Not without a bunk. I refuse to sit on the ground like an animal.

GUARD
Get in the cell.

(She pushes her, but Ana resists, sitting just outside the light.)

ANA
A chair, at least. Something so I'm not on the floor all the time.

GUARD
You're on the floor now.

ANA
I need a chair.

(Guard raises her baton to beat her, then smiles, lowering it. She goes off. Ana hugs herself. Guard returns, carrying a chair. She steps into the square of light, setting it down.)

GUARD
There's your chair.

(Ana rises, holding onto her pants with one hand.)

ANA
Thank you.

(Guard nods, then grabs a hold of the chair and removes it. She walks out of the light. The cell door clangs shut. Ana lunges for the edge of the lit space. Guard's laughter rings out.)

ANA
You bitch! You fucking, cock sucking,
(Searching for the worst thing she can think of)
--middle class whore!

(Her string of obscenities is greeted by more laughter. Ana slumps down on her mattress, shivering, rocking and holding herself.)

ANA
It's okay; you're going to be okay. It's going to be –

(She freezes. Softly, from off stage, come the sounds of women singing☺

WOMEN (O.S.)
Me quiero casar / Con una senorita / que sepa border / con esta si –
ANA
(Joins in with their voices)
con esta no / con esta senorita, me caso you!

(She laughs, then a sob catches in her throat, then cries softly. Lights slowly condense on her.)

ANA
Oscar Wilde said, "A day in prison when we don't cry is a day in which the heart hardens, not a day in which one feels well."

(She searches her pockets and comes out with a hanky, blows her nose. Examines the hanky.)

Teresa's work. When did she -- ? She must have slipped it into my pocket before I left them. Such tiny stitches. Delicate. It smells of Teresa. Strong. Even ill she has the presence to think of others.

At the military barracks, where I was before here, I did more than 200 days of solitary. You can get sent to the calabozo for disobeying a direct order or for singing a "subversive song." Or, like me, for writing a letter revealing a tiny truth about life here. Prison life we can adjust to. There are others to help you through. Things to fill your days – even the work in the fields or the kitchen are something. We have our crafts; we have study groups, plays to perform from time to time. Visits to look forward to every other week, unless you get sanctioned. Which I do. Often. But in here – it's hard. No books, just a few basic items.

(She reaches down and takes up her cloth bag, opening it. Holding it up, she displays her number.)

548. That's me. But not me.
(Takes out items and lines up neatly on the floor in front of her)

ANA (CONT.)
Toothpaste. Toothbrush. Toilet paper. Soap. Rose scented.
Not mine. Maybe Susana slipped it in or Maria.
(Digging in bag, then bringing out wool socks)
An extra pair of socks. Again, Teresa's work. And that's -- all.
(Shakes out the bag)
It's cold in here, so cold, so they dressed me in layers. No hats
or gloves allowed but they allow us to layer our clothing.
Ridiculous rules.

*(She stands up, does a few jumping jacks, walks across her light, then
back, then across again.*
Knocking is heard coming from O.S.

*Ana walks along the perimeter of the light, feeling the "walls". There is a
series of knocks. She squats, putting her ear against the "wall". She
knocks: "Ciao" – 3 knocks, pause, 9 knocks, pause, 1 knock, pause,
16 knocks (less than "hola"). There is a response O.S.: 3 knocks,
pause, 9 knocks, pause, 1 knock, pause.)*

Ciao! A compañeras. She wants to talk. It's the same
everywhere -- even in solitary, we find ways to communicate
with each other. Every knock stands for a letter. One knock
is "A", two knocks "B", and so on.

*There are a series of knocks O.S. Ana listens attentively, using her
fingers to keep track: Six knocks, pause . . . Ana bursts out laughing.*

She says, "Fuck the dog."

(She taps "yes" back.)

She wants to know what I'm accused of. Now, that, that's a
sensitive question. She must be fairly new. Poor thing. See,
you never admit to anything in here. You never know who
you're talking to. And even if she can be trusted under, shall I
say, "normal circumstances," who's to say what she'll reveal if
pressed? Or, like Lidia, she just wants to make life easier on
herself. Lidia, another dog.

ANA (CONT.)
She'd sell you out for an extra shower.
(There's more knocking, softly, though, so as not too distract.)
I try to remember not everyone's like Lidia.
(She sniffs handkerchief)
During my interrogation they asked me, did I do this, was I
involved in that? I simply stated, "Neither yes nor no, and the
reverse of both." I held that statement in my mouth, my lips
and tongue repeating it, even after they quit asking. "Neither
yes nor no, and the reverse of both." I thought I was pretty
clever. Apparently, not clever enough.

(She gestures to the space she's in.)

I will admit this, though, everything I did I did because I
believed in it. Not because my lover believed in it, but because
I truly believed – I believe – this is a beautiful country that
deserves better. But in the cold of a cell, when you get a letter
stating that your father asked for you-- before he died, and that
you never got to say goodbye, well, then doubt begins to seep
in like the cold through the floor of the calabozo. It's hard to
shake sometimes it. But even then, even then I hold firm to
one belief that has only gotten stronger since I've been here: I
will always believe in the beauty and compassion of mis
compañeras.
(Shouts, pumping her fist, the hanky waving in it)
Hasta siempre, Compañeras! Hasta siempre!

(Lights dim and go out on her as knocking O.S. continues.)

THE END.

26 LAS SOLDADERAS
drama/oral interpretation

I discovered las soldaderas when asked by the University of North Dakota Women's Center to write a piece for Cinco de Mayo. The first thing I learned was that Cinco de Mayo, contrary to common belief in the U.S., is not Mexico's independence day; that would be Sept. 16th. I began playing with other erroneous beliefs non-Mexicans might have about Mexicans, which led me to research women's roles in Mexican history. The first thing I came across were these revolutionary women who fought alongside the men for almost ten years, 1910-1919. They were in combat, sometimes disguised as men, but often not. Remember: women did not have the right to vote in the U.S. at this time. The story of the women of the Mexican Revolution has often been sexualized to the point of their becoming pin-up girls. Here is part of their story in all its raw brutality and courage.

CHARACTERS:

ISABEL – part of the narrating team
LISA – part of the narrating team, performs as ANGELA JIMINEZ – dressed as a woman with bandoliers across her chest
RACHEL – part of the narrating team, performs as PEDRO/PETRA RUIZ, dressed as a male soldier
THERESA – part of the narrating team, performs as BEARIZ ORTEGA de GONZALEZ, dressed as a traditional Mexican woman

TECH requirements: You will need to locate images of "Adelita" and perhaps also las Soldaderas to project during the performance. These are easily located on the Internet.

The premiere performance staged the women around the room and had them interact with the audience. Each woman took center stage during her monologue.

TIME: Today

ISABEL *(in Spanish)*:
When you think of Mexicans, what comes to mind?
(images projected)
All Mexican women are maids?
All Mexican guys are in construction?
The teenagers are gangsters?
Mexican families pick your food?
And any Mexican in America is a border jumper?

THE WOMEN step forward, taking turns – *(In English)*
They're greasy,
they're dirty,
they're lazy,
they're drunks,
they have huge families
and drive old cars,
swallow the worm
and eat the taco,
wear a sombrero
and ride a burro
and listen to mariachi.
And the women – ay! Caramba!
Oh, and if you have a garage sale this summer, be careful because those Mejicanos will chisel you down!

ISABEL
We only have an hour, so we can't dismantle every stereotype, or myth.

RACHEL
But let's start with one: Cinco de Mayo is not Mexican
Independence Day. That would be Sept. 16th. Cinco de Mayo
marks the Battle of Puebla in 1862 when the Mexican army
defeated the French in an unlikely victory. So, there you go.
Thank you and good night.
(they all start to leave)

LISA
More? Okay, but I have another appointment and I wouldn't
want to show up late on Mexican time. Let's talk about las
soldaderas. We begin with
Adelita.
(song begins to play & images are shown)

LISA *(cont.)*
Adelita is the focus of a corrido, a type of Mexican ballad,
usually about history, oppression, los campesinos. You know,
"power to the people."
(Raises a fist)
Intiende? Bueno. "Adelita" idolizes una soldadera, and in fact,
"Adelita" <u>became</u> the archetype for las soladeras.

She is a warrior, but they always emphasize that she's a woman
first. They want to remind you that she has tetas not cojones.
Look! Her blouses can barely contain her breasts! And many
images have her wearing bullets for a bra.
(Slide show as song plays)

Here's a translation of the song all los campesinos know:

The bugle sounds, to announce the war
the brave warrior comes out to fight
rivers of blood will flow
a tyrant in power, never

RACHEL
And if I died in battle
and if my body will lie in the ground
Adelita for God's sake I beg you
don't cry for me

THERESA
Don't cry anymore my dear Adelita
don't cry my dear woman
don't be ungrateful with me
don't make me suffer

ISABEL
I say goodbye now, my dear Adelita
I will go away with great pleasure
I carry your picture in my chest
like a shield, to win every battle

LISA
Wait! I thought that was a song about a woman who was a revolutionary? Sounds more like the guy's the focus of the song called "Adelita"!

RACHEL
Yes, a common depiction is Adelita, as the helpmate of the soldier. This is a role everyone is comfortable with., but las soldaderas were that and so much more.

ISABEL
See, Adelita is not based on a real woman. She may be a composite of helpmates during the Revolution. She may just be pure fantasy. We don't know.

LISA
Here's what we do know: Las soldaderas did exist and they served in the Mexican Revolution as soldiers between 1910 and 1919.

THERESA
But first, what is this word "soldadera"? During the Mexican Revolution men received a salary, soldada. They often gave that salary to a woman, sometimes their wife, a sister, or a single woman who followed the troops. She spent it on food, carried his bedding for him, and cooked his meals. Hence, these women became known as soldaderas.

LISA
Sometimes a woman did not have any choice. Soldiers would often kidnap women.

ISABEL
Hold on, now. Sometimes the soldiers gave the women a choice: join us or we kill you.

RACHEL
How very liberal.

THERESA
It wasn't just bands of soldiers who forced women, either. Sometimes a woman's husband would expect her to follow him into war to take care of him. A famous US journalist John Reed once asked a soldier why his wife had to also go and fight for Madero's army, and he responded by saying, "Shall I starve then? Who shall make my tortillas but my woman?"

RACHEL
Among the types of soldaderas were the help-mates and the prostitutes. Both roles sound traditional, but actually both were pushing the boundaries of conventional roles for women. The prostitutes were attempting to take control of their bodies.

LISA
Oh, please.

THERESA
It's true. As you will hear, rape was as common as killing during la Revolution. A woman who sold her body was part of the troop. She took refuge with that troop. They paid her, fed her, and protected her from enemy soldiers.

LISA
Hello? In return she traded her body. She wasn't particularly loyal, either. If the troop was overcome by the enemy and she survived, she simply "enlisted" with the enemy, offering her services to him. Free enterprise at its finest.

RACHEL
But even the help-mates were living outside the box of conventionality. There was more freedom on the battle trail than there was at home.

THERESA
Women were an essential part of las Revolution and they knew it. Had the women not accompanied the men, many historians believe that the men would have deserted.

LISA
Remember, these are guerilla militias with no infrastructure. Women provided food, shelter, medical care, and comfort.

ISABEL
Enough with the yakking. Vamanos, let's meet several women who existed during the Mexican Revolution.
Primero, the helpmate.

BEATRIZ
Yo soy Beatriz Gonzalez Oretega. Pancho Villa did not like having women around. He said, it slowed down his troops. But the fact is he needed us or the men would abandon him. We made war tolerable by going ahead and setting up camp, starting the fire, preparing the food.

BEATRIZ (CONT.)
We weren't treated well. The horses were treated better. When we traveled by train, which we often did, the horses rode in the cars, the women on top of the cars. We were, how you say? "Sitting ducks" for the enemy.

As bad as it was, it was better than staying at home, where insurgents often raped women or the federales – raping women was something all the men seemed to agree upon. Every social class was kidnapped.

Even those who had taken Holy Orders were not safe: The Carrancistas captured fifty nuns. After a certain amount of time passed, they dropped them off at a hospital -- where they bore their offspring.

If we weren't raped and or murdered, we were kidnapped. No. Better to follow the men you knew. That felt like a choice when women had very few choices. A Mexican woman was seen – is often still seen -- as either the bad girl or the good girl – a virgin. I (curtsy) was the virgin *(winks)*.

LISA
Yeah, me, too!

BEATRIZ
Or, at least, that's how it's been recorded in history. And we all know: history never lies. Pero, I digress. I am Beatriz Gonzalez Ortega. If you travel in Mexico you will hear my name. Many schools are named after me because of what I did during la Revolution. A small thing to me, the right thing, but they made it into a big thing. I tended the sick.

Like so many other soladeras. I served as a nurse. Pero, I nursed them all. If a federales was brought in, much as I might despise what he stood for, he was still a human being suffering. I did what I could for him. A Zapista? I tended his wounds. A Villalista? The same.

BEATRIZ (CONT.)
Despite the uniform we wear, we all bleed. We all feel pain.
The first time they caught me tending the enemy, I was
scolded, beaten even. I promised I'd never do it again.
Entonces, in the future, the first thing I did when I met with
an injured man? Cut off his uniform. Then I burned it. It's
hard to tell who is the ally and who is the enemy without the
uniform: A naked man is a naked man.
(Turning away, then turns back, smiling)
Si, some are smaller, some are bigger, but in war? *(Now sober)*
They all cry.

ISABEL
Beatriz Ortega de Gonzalez, ladies and gentlemen. Remember
her name. Beatriz was rebellious, but still very traditional.
There were also those who were less so. I present – Angela
Jiminez

ANGELA
My sister Maria was 17. I was 16. Neither of us was married.
There were boys, though, whom we had our eyes on and who
had their eyes on us. But when the Revolution began, the boys
went away to join the fight. After that, we would talk for
hours, late into the night, about when our brave boys came
home and the grand fiesta we would have. Our wedding day,
how we would have a double wedding, las dos hermanas y dos
caballeros. We'd argue over who would bring the first grand
child into the world – Maria or me. She teased me that with
the size of my hips, I'd pop out triplets before she could
squeeze out one. We laughed in the bed we shared until mama
would yell from the next room: Be quiet and go to sleep,
muchachas! I'd often wake up with her curled around my
body. Keeping me warm. Protecting me. Mi Hermana.

But then the Federales came, like a pack of dogs in the night.
It was clear, they had not just come to raid our village, steal
our food and guns, kill whatever old man was left. They came
to rape the girls and women. Young, old, it did not matter to
them. No woman was safe. Funny, they saw themselves as –

ANGELA (CONT.)

--patriots but they were just perverts. Maria and I ran, she into the shed, I behind some barrels behind it. What happened next I did not see, but I heard. I heard her screams, heard her begging, heard him call her a dirty peasant whore – then his laughter, then 2 shots. Maria must have gotten a hold of his pistol. One bullet was for him, one for herself.

What choice did I have? I joined my father to avenge my sister's death. But I was not going to carry any man's mattress or make his tortillas. No. I disguised myself as man, for even the soldaderas were not safe from the abuse of the very men they traveled with.

I was a good shot, and soon proved myself as a worthy soldier. I served with several rebel troops, eventually achieving the rank of Lieutenant Colonel, earning the respect of my troops but always fighting for my sisters. Las hermanas siempre. Viva la revolución!

ISABEL

Lt. Colonel Angela Jiminez! Bueno. Angela was not the only noteworthy soldier during la Revolución. May I introduce you to "El Echa Balas" – the Bullet Slinger.

PEDRO/PETRA

Some knew me as Pedro Ruiz. I was born in Acapulco in 1893. Rape is part of my story, as well. I was an orphan living in Guerrero when military forces raped me. Have you ever seen a cock fight? Where the men stand around cheering their bird on? That's what I remember. A circle of men, cheering each other on as they took turns raping me.

A woman is so vulnerable in life, so I chose not to be a woman. I cut my hair, I wore men's trousers, and I allowed myself to give into the violence all around me. Violence springs from a desire to control – other men, women, animals, land, the rules – I want it my way or else I will hurt you.

PEDRO/PETRA (CONT.)

My violence, however, was directed at the enemy. Women could never be my enemy. Even if I chose not to live my life as a woman, women were to be cherished. Like my compadres, I chased the ladies. Often, the women did not know my true self. They swooned in my arms as they did for any man in uniform. And when they closed their eyes, and their long black, eyelashes rested on their cheeks, my desire was as strong as any man's in my unit. A kiss from a woman's lips was the only thing that briefly softened me.

Sometimes a woman would guess at my disguise. Sometimes what I lacked made no difference. Or – all the difference.
But I never took a woman by force. I could wield a knife at the enemy, insert it into his gut and twist it around, but a woman's body is sacred.

After I'd achieved the rank of Lieutenant my battalion took control of a hacienda while fighting in Oaxaca. The owner was killed and some soldiers were arguing over who would be the first to rape the owner's 15-year old daughter. I heard her screaming so I said, "I'm taking this one, and if any of you don't like it, you can tangle with me!" I hauled her up on my horse as she beat my back with her fists.

Once we got away from the rest, I stopped, dismounted and pulled her to the ground. "Don't be afraid," I said. I unbuttoned my shirt to reveal my breasts, bound tightly to be sure, but definitely breasts. "I am a woman, too. Now run! Run as fast as you can!"

The look on her face was – confusion, relief, and had we met under different circumstances – I think we might have gotten to know each other better. (*winks*)
Toward the end of the war, our new President Carranza was reviewing the troops, as he walked past, I stepped forward. "Mr. President, since there's no more fighting, I want to ask for my discharge from the army, but first I want you to know that a woman has served you as a soldier."

PEDRO/PETRA (CONT.)
Petra Ruiz. But you can call me Pedro.

THERESA
In Puente de Ixtla, Morelos, the widows, wives, daughters and sisters of the rebels formed their own battalion to 'seek vengeance for the dead.' Under the command of a stocky former tortilla-maker by the name of China, they carried out incursions throughout the Tetecala district. Some dressed in rags, others in elegant stolen clothes--silk stockings and silk dresses, huaraches, straw hats and cartridge belts--these women became the terror of the region. Others – preferred the dress of men.

LISA
Out of a population of 15 million at the beginning of the Revolution, as many as 2 million people died or left the country before the fighting ended--1 out of 7!

RACHEL
With its current population of 300 million, the US would have to lose 40 million to compare in percentage of loss.

ISABEL
On the positive side, Mexicans freed themselves from a dictatorship propped up by a feudal aristocracy based in the haciendas, and from foreign corporations that dominated much of Mexico's industry and resources.

LISA
Workers gained undreamed of rights,

RACHEL
--campesinos won the right to own the land they tilled,

THERESA
--and the status of women improved immensely—

ISABEL
--although there was still a long way to go.

ALL
Viva la revolución!!

THE END.

27 "Club Sandwich"
comedy/mild language, sexual references

Time: Present

Place: Foyer with adjoining guest room in home.

Characters:

Alice - woman in her 40s-early 50s, has the patience of a saint, gentle heart, but about to lose it.

Muriel - woman in her 70s, feisty despite a broken ankle. Alice's stepmother.

Audra - woman in her 70s, equally as feisty but perhaps not as likeable as Muriel. Alice's mother.

There is a "guest room" on one side of the stage, which includes two recliners separated by an end table. MURIEL is sits in the chair, s.r.. One ankle is propped up on a pillow. It is in a cast up to the knee. She rings a small brass bell. There is no immediate response, so she rings again. S.L. is a foyer with the entry off-stage.

(ALICE enters carrying a tray with a bowl and a glass of water on it. Her hair is moderately disheveled. Her blouse is untucked.)

MURIEL
(slurs her words, just a bit)
There you are, darling, I woke up with such a patched mouth.

ALICE
A parched mouth? I brought you some soup –

MURIEL
So dry. Maybe it's the pain medication?

ALICE
Could be.
(Alice sets the tray up on Muriel's lap.)

MURIEL
I hope I'm not addicted. Edna Shlosky in 9-A became a drug addict when she broke her hip.

ALICE
It's only been 24-hours, Muriel. You can't possibly have become addicted.

MURIEL
I know, but I like the way it makes me feel. That can't be good.

ALICE
How does it make you feel?

MURIEL
Like I've had three Bloody Marys in a row.

ALICE
Sounds nice.

MURIEL
Ummm, it is. Help yourself, dear.

ALICE
That'd be illegal.

MURIEL
So, now I'm a pusher? I like that. I'm high and a pusher. At 70 I didn't think there was any mischief left to bake. I mean make.
ALICE
Do you need anything else? I've got to get some paper work done.

MURIEL
Oh, I'll be fine, darling. The soap smells delicious.

ALICE
Just ring if you need anything else.
(She exits "room" as Muriel raises her glass to her.)

(The DOOR BELL rings. Alice moves to answer it, but before she can get there, a door slams and Audra enters.)

AUDRA
I hear you got her here.

ALICE
Mother, I –

AUDRA
Meant to call me? I am trying hard not to take this as a betrayal because I know how manipulative she is.

ALICE
Shh! She'll hear you.

AUDRA
I hope she hears me, slut!

MURIEL
Is that Audra?

ALICE
She didn't have anyone to turn to. No friends, no children.

AUDRA
And whose fault is that? Home wrecker! No, you should have let her go to a nursing home.

ALICE
She broke her ankle!

AUDRA
Exactly. You can't take care of her here. Look, I know a nursing home on Cherry. They supposedly got rid of the bed bugs. She'll get the care she deserves. It's cheap.

ALICE
You forget: I like Muriel.

AUDRA
Why?

(Muriel RINGS bell).

ALICE
I have to go.

AUDRA
But we're having a conversation. Alice, I'm speaking to you!

(Alice goes to Muriel's room; Audra follows her.)

MURIEL
I'm sorry, darling – Oh. Audra. How -- nice to see you!

AUDRA
Muriel.

ALICE
Mother stopped by to see how you're doing.

MURIEL
Did she? Your daughter was sweet to take me sin.

AUDRA
She does things like that. Stray cats, fallen birds. Even caught spiders in jars and freed them <u>outside</u> the house.

ALICE
Mother, that's —

MURIEL
That's okay, darling. It's sad how Audra never got over the fat your father left her — for me.
AUDRA
He didn't leave. He was stolen.

ALICE
Please, that was forty-five years ago!

AUDRA
Forty-five and a half!

MURIEL
Water under the ridge.

AUDRA
He was a married man with a sickly child.

ALICE
I wasn't sickly.

AUDRA
You had allergies and a nasty over-bite.

MURIEL
Alice, I never meant to make tubble for you.

ALICE
You're not. Mother, must you?

AUDRA
Do what? I didn't sleep with a married man. I wasn't a home wrecker. There's a special ring in hell for women like you.

MURIEL
How many times do I have to tell you – he told me he was divorced!

AUDRA
So you say. And you're slurring. Did she have a stroke? If she had a stroke you cannot keep her here, Alice. I bet she had a stroke.

ALICE
She didn't have a stroke. It's the pain pills. Maybe you should go now.

AUDRA
Fine. I just stopped by to see if Leonora was telling the truth: My daughter took in a harlot.

MURIEL
I am no hornet! Damn. She's making me lose my buzz.
(She pops a pill.)

ALICE
Muriel, I don't think you should –

MURIEL
Down the hatch!

ALICE
Okay, Mother, thanks for stopping. Call you later.
(Alice firmly turns Audra and heads her out.)

AUDRA
My daughter is a pushover! She should kick you to the curb!

MURIEL
(Gives her the Italian hand gesture for you know what)
When you get a chance, Alice, a little salt, please. This soap needs a little salt.

In the foyer.

AUDRA
My daughter's soup never needs salt!

ALICE
Ta-ta.

AUDRA
What? Now I can't visit my own daughter?

ALICE
You came here to chew her out – again. 45-years and Dad's been gone ten. Don't you think it's time to bury it?

AUDRA
Love to. I'll even pay for her coffin.

ALICE
Call you tomorrow. *(Alice gently shoves her off-stage.)*

AUDRA
She deserves to be in a nursing home! Not my daughter's home!

(Muriel RINGS bell.)

ALICE
Toodles. Oh, wa-wa-watch –

AUDRA (O.S.)
Jee-sus, Mary, and ---!

ALICE
Mother! *(She rushes off-stage.)*

LIGHTS.

(In the dark a bell rings, followed by one of a different tone, followed insistently by the first one, followed by . . .)

LIGHTS UP.

(Audra is now in the second chair, Muriel in the first. The night table separates them. There are more bottles of pills on the table. Both women are ringing their bells at each other. Alice enters, hair really messy, clothing looks like it hasn't been changed in a few days.)

ALICE
I'm here, please, *please*, just stop ringing.

AUDRA
She started.

MURIEL
I need another pwillow to elevate my ankle, darling.

AUDRA
I need one, too. I like to have my head above my heart.

MURIEL
I didn't know you had one.

AUDRA
Harlot!

MURIEL
Bitch!

(Alice turns away, sniffling.)

MURIEL
Darling? Are you crying?

AUDRA
What's wrong, dear? Is it too much for you? If it is, Muriel can go to a nursing home.

ALICE
All the *ringing*. I have this deadline, and with all the ringing, I can't concentrate. If you could somehow, I don't know, hold your requests and I can fill them all at once?

MURIEL
Certainly, darling. We've been inconwiderate.

AUDRA
What if I have to go wee?

ALICE
Well, then, of course, ring. It's just —

MURIEL
If you must wee, get your water and your willow fluffed at the same time.

ALICE
Exactly.

AUDRA
So, what? Now I'm the demanding one? And she's a — a — saint?

ALICE
Oh, Mother . . .

AUDRA
As if she's one to talk? "Alice, get me the bed pan!" "Alice, get me a cup of coffee!" "Alice, I need another pain killer!"

MURIEL
I have been the perfect patient, which is more than I can say
for you.

AUDRA
Home wrecker!

MURIEL
He told me he was diworced!

ALICE
Please! I – I – can't take it anymore! 23 years of this
squabbling, always tugging me one way, then another, are my
arms longer than a normal person's because they should be!
I've always felt lucky to have both of you in my life, but right
now I am ready to throw you into the back of my hatchback
and dump you at the nursing home. So – so – so knock it off
already! Or – else!
(Stomps off)

MURIEL
She's a good girl.

AUDRA
The best part of her father.

*(Muriel nods, opens up a bottle of pills and takes two out. She hands one
to Audra.)*

AUDRA
Oo, your private stock?

MURIEL
This is the good stuff. Take two. It's like thwee Bloody Marys
in a wow.
(Raising her glass)
To Alice.

(They clink glasses. Both down the pills and drink.)

MURIEL
You know, I wasn't the first and I wasn't the last. Chester was a cheater. He cheated on you, and when he cheated on me.

AUDRA
You?

MURIEL
Our darling Chester couldn't keep his pecker in his pants.

AUDRA
I had crabs the first year we were married.

MURIEL
See?

AUDRA
He told me I must have caught it off the toilet seat at Schotenstein's.

MURIEL
Gave me the clap.

AUDRA
No! Nasty.

MURIEL
So? Why you smiling?

AUDRA
Am I? Sorry. You know, all these wears, I mean years, I've been so angry at you, that I never stopped to consider I was better off without him.

MURIEL
You were. Gambled, drank, womanized.

AUDRA
I should thank you.

MURIEL
I did you a favor.

AUDRA
Yes, yes, maybe you did.

MURIEL
You're welcome.

AUDRA
Thank you.

MURIEL
He wasn't even that good in bed.
(*Audra gives her a look*)
Except when he was sober. Then that man --

AUDRA
Enough.

MURIEL
He was hardly ever sober.

AUDRA
He wasn't even a good fatter.

MURIEL
A bum.

AUDRA
A loser with a capital "Loo."

AUDRA & MURIEL
May he west in peace.
(*They cross themselves.*)

THE END.

28 Women with Wrinkles

a one-act play

Time: Today, late morning

Place: A nursing home recreation room in Louisiana. The home is somewhat run down, with ratty chairs, and a small television, d.s.l.

Characters:

VIOLA THIBIDOUX - a 74-year old, white, Southern woman, perhaps Scarlet O'Hara as a senior citizen.

BERTY ROBINSON - a spirited, intelligent, Southern, black woman, in her late 70s.

ROBIN – male or female, an orderly who cares about the residents but it's basically just a job and there are other things s/he'd rather be doing. Age is not relevant, although s/he should be a good bit younger than the residents.

Scene 1

(VIOLA seated in a wheel chair next to the table s.c. The table is littered with dog-eared magazines.)

(VIOLA is dressed up, complete with a handbag and a shawl, which hangs precariously down on her left side. She is fast asleep.

The walls of the nursing home are hung with Halloween decorations. ROBIN wheels in BERTY, who is also dressed up in her Sunday best. ROBIN where's a hospital smock over her/his clothes, and "nurse's" shoes. She has on a name tag, and some papers protrude from her rear pocket.)

BERTY
They said they'd be here shortly after lunch.

ROBIN
I'm sure they will.
(scribbles some notes on the papers she takes from her pocket)

BERTY
You be sure and tell them I'm in here. 'Cause they'll go to my room.

ROBIN
I'll tell them.

BERTY
Well, don't just tell them. Show them, for Pete's sake! What are we paying you for!

ROBIN
(Wheeling to other side of table)
I'll show 'em, Miss Berty.

BERTY
Good. 'Cause otherwise they might get lost. And if Charles gets lost he might not find me. He might think I've gone out or something.

ROBIN
Now, where would he think you'd have gone?

BERTY
Don't get smart with me! My Charles gets frustrated real easy.
So, you just show him where I'm at, and that's that. Nice and
simple. You got that?

ROBIN
Yes, Miss BERTY. Here you go.

BERTY
Who the heck is that?

ROBIN
She's new. Name's Viola Thibidoux. Now you behave
yourself and I'll see you later with your pills.
(*She exits*)

BERTY
Hey, don't set me next to---

*BERTY looks over at VIOLA, who is still fast asleep. Her shawl is
hanging real low on the side closest to BERTY. BERTY shrugs, looks
around stealthily, and reaches into her dress pocket. She removes a piece of
Halloween candy. Slowly she unwraps it, every once in awhile VIOLA
will stir, as though she's heard the noise. Finally, BERTY finishes the
unwrapping of the candy and pops one in her mouth.*

BERTY
Umm...sugar. Nobody gonna tell me what I can and can't eat.

*(She then reaches for a magazine. She flips thru, then finds an article and
begins to read.*

*VIOLA begins to emit a series of loud snores. BERTY becomes
increasingly annoyed and reaches out and nudges VIOLA. This jars the
shawl, and it slips completely to the ground. BERTY, struggling to reach
it, bangs the table and wakes up VIOLA.)*

VIOLA
Rudolph? What? What?
(She sees BERTY with her shawl)
Thief! Thief!
(Ringing her bell)
Orderly come quick, I say! I been robbed!

BERTY
Hush now, you old fool. I'm not robbing nothing.

VIOLA
Liar, that is my shawl!

BERTY
I know. It fell. I picked it up. Now, take it and hush up.

VIOLA
It fell did it? And I suppose you expect me to believe that? If I hadn't woken up when I did my shawl would have been history.

BERTY
I resent being called a thief!

VIOLA
You've been coveting this shawl as I sat hear napping, haven't you? I see that look in your eye. Why you've been absolutely green with envy. And so should you be. Even you can see the quality. Pure, virgin lambs wool from England. So soft, so finely knit. My mama made this, Lord rest her soul. She wore it round her shoulders, as she rocked her babies every evening. When she died I put it away in a cedar chest. I knew one day I'd find comfort in it in my old age. And I have. And you think you can steal it? Well you got another thing coming!
(VIOLA shakes a fist at her)

BERTY
Don't you raise your hand to me, you senile old bitty!

VIOLA
You Negroes always stealing from us whites!

BERTY
You whites always blaming us for everything that's ever been missing. And I ain't no thief!

VIOLA
You is, and I am letting it be known.
        (Ringing bell)
Orderly! Orderly!

BERTY
Fine, and I'm letting it be known that you are ready to be moved to the insane asylum! ROBIN!

BERTY glances at VIOLA, then looks more closely at VIOLA's dress. She plucks at the material.

VIOLA
Don't you touch me!
BERTY
That's my dress!

VIOLA
I beg your pardon!?

BERTY
It is! You are wearing my dress!

VIOLA
This is my dress!

BERTY
It is not, why look it's even too big on you.

(VIOLA glances down. The chest is indeed too large.)

VIOLA
It must have stretched.

BERTY
Yeah, it stretched from your closet to mine! What you doing
in my dress? You going in my closet?

VIOLA
I would not venture in your closet for the life of me!

BERTY
My, my, my don't your children by you any clothes?

VIOLA
This is not your dress, you ridiculous old fool!

BERTY
Oh, really?
        (grabbing bell)
Robin! Oh, Robin!

(ROBIN enters from s.r.)

ROBIN
What's all the fuss in here?

VIOLA
She stole my shawl!

BERTY
She stole my dress!

VIOLA
Did not!

BERTY
Did too!

ROBIN
Okay, okay, this can be resolved real easily. Miss Viola, if you'll allow me, I'll just see whose name is printed inside the collar.

VIOLA
By all means.
(She bows her head)

ROBIN
Let's see here, it says...Alberta ROBINson.

BERTY
Ah ha!

VIOLA
But that can't be! It was in my closet this morning!

BERTY
Well it is. Now take it off.

VIOLA
How could a thing like this happen?

ROBIN
I'm sorry, Miss Viola. Sometimes there's a mix up in the laundry. The wrong items get sent to the wrong patients. You just return the dress to the laundry and Miss Berty will get it back when it's washed. No big deal.

VIOLA
No big deal? No big deal!?

BERTY
I want it back now!

VIOLA
Robin, you don't seem to understand. I am wearing an old, Negro woman's dress.

ROBIN
Yes?

VIOLA
On my flesh!

ROBIN
Uh-huh.

VIOLA
Robin, against my --- bosom.

BERTY
Take it off right now, I say!

VIOLA
In all my years, I have never been so - so-

BERTY
You dare call me thief when you steal my good dress. I have a
good mind to call the police! I think I will! Police! Police!

VIOLA
Hush! Just hush! Oh, ROBIN take me to my room, I can't
see my family wearing this- this - dress!

ROBIN
Okay, okay, everyone just calm down! We don't need to over
react, Miss Berty!

BERTY
Police!

(ROBIN begins pushing VIOLA off.)

VIOLA
This would never have happened at St. Augustine's Home!
Never!

BERTY
Thief!
(takes out a candy, unwraps it, pops it in her mouth.)
Umm...How sweet it is!

LIGHTS

Scene 2

(Later that day. BERTY is seated in the same place. ROBIN wheels in VIOLA. She pushes her to the same spot.)

VIOLA
(stage whisper)
Don't set me by her!

ROBIN
But there's nobody else in here.

VIOLA
I do not care. Set me as far from her as you can. Over in that corner will be just fine.

BERTY
How 'bout in the next wing!

ROBIN
Now, Miss BERTY, that's not very nice. After all, Miss Viola is new here.

VIOLA
I won't be here long, though.

ROBIN
You girls should try and get to know each other. Let bygones be bygones.
(She wheels VIOLA right over to the table)
Come on, Miss Bertie. It was just a laundry mix up.

BERTY
She called me a thief, too. Or did you forget that? I suppose it doesn't matter much if a white woman calls a colored woman a thief, does it? Oh, but if a white woman steals something from a black woman, then it's a mix-up is it? That how it is around here, Robin?

ROBIN
You know that's not true, Miss Berty. You two try and talk and maybe I'll let you stay up a little later tonight. Hmm?

BERTY
So's I can watch Matlock?

ROBIN
Maybe. If you two make up. *(Exits)* See you later, then.

(BERTY and VIOLA glare at each other. They both try very hard to wheel their chairs away from the table, but both give up exhausted after a few beats.)

VIOLA
I do not care to talk to you. I do not watch Matlock, and have never cared for that Andy Griffith, anyways.

BERTY
What's there not to like about Andy Griffith?

VIOLA
He's too---nice.

BERTY
How can somebody be too nice?

VIOLA
I don't know how somebody can be too nice, but Andy Griffith sure has accomplished it. "Oh, Oppie son...Oh, Aunt Bea...Oh, Gomer, haw, haw, haw, gosh oh gee" Yep, just too darn nice, if you ask me.

BERTY
And I suppose you think Santa Claus is a fool, too?

VIOLA
Listen, you, just don't speak to me, and everything will be fine.

BERTY
My pleasure.

(ROBIN enters.)

ROBIN
Bad news, Miss Viola. Your son just called and he won't be visiting you today, after all. Said something unexpected came up at the office.

VIOLA
Oh? Wonder what that was?

ROBIN
Didn't say, ma'am.

BERTY
Did my son call?

ROBIN
No, Miss Berty.

BERTY
He said he'd be here by 1 o'clock.

ROBIN
          (Exiting)
I'll let you know if he calls.

VIOLA
According to my watch it is 4 o'clock now.

BERTY
Well, thank you Miss Time Keeper. Besides, I thought we weren't talking to each other.

VIOLA
We aren't, so hush up. Maybe the reason your son isn't coming is because you talk so much.

BERTY
You don't know if my son isn't coming! He is often late. He is a very busy man.

VIOLA
So is my son, but at least he had the decency to call.

BERTY
Well, my son didn't call because he's probably on his way. But your son called, and he ain't coming. So, just hush your mouth.

VIOLA
My son isn't coming because he is a very important man. He has very important things to do. And he lives in Baton Rouge. That's three hours away from here.

BERTY
Did you ever wonder why your son would but you in a nursing home three hours away from where he lives?

VIOLA
Oh---just hush yourself!

BERTY
Don't tell me to hush, you hush!

ROBIN
(*Enters with tray of pills and two small cups of water*)
Here we go ladies, pop a couple of these and you'll be great
pals before long. Let's see, three for you, Miss Viola and --
eight for you, Miss Berty.

BERTY
How come she gets three and I have to take eight?

VIOLA
'Cause I'm a lot healthier than you. Isn't that so, Robin?

BERTY
Maybe it's 'cause you're a lost cause.

ROBIN
No, no, you both have different needs is all.

BERTY
Oh? Wouldn't have anything to do with her being white,
would it?

ROBIN
Sorry? I don't quite follow that.

BERTY
Well, these things cost something, don't they?

ROBIN
Of course.

BERTY
So, you wouldn't be giving me sugar tablets and charging my
son for them? The white establishment has always hated
colored folks with money.

ROBIN
No, Miss BERTY, they are not sugar tablets. They are pills
that you need to keep you healthy.

VIOLA
Isn't that just like colored folks, to turn every little thing into a race issue?

BERTY
Maybe, because to you folks, everything is a race issue!

ROBIN
Now, now ladies, calm down. Take your pills like good girls. Go on, down the hatch, Miss Viola

VIOLA
Don't you treat me like a child!

ROBIN
If you all are gonna act like children I am going to treat you all like children. Now take your pills. Miss Berty?

BERTY
She's right, don't treat us like little children. We are grown women, and if we don't want to take our pills you can't make us.

VIOLA
She can't?

BERTY
No, she can't. Residents have rights, you know?

VIOLA
I didn't know! Well fine. I don't want to take this one.

BERTY
I got that one, too. Gives you the runs, doesn't it?

VIOLA
Well, it sure enough does.

BERTY
So, I'm not going to take it.
(She tosses it across the room)
VIOLA
Me either!
(She tosses hers)

ROBIN
Stop that this instant!

BERTY
I don't want that one either, or that one!
(Tosses each one)

ROBIN
You all have gone off the deep end! There will be no *Matlock* for either of you!

VIOLA
I hate that Andy Griffith anyway!
(She tosses out a pill)

BERTY
Yeah, he is a little too wimpy!
(Tosses another out)

ROBIN
Fine! Just fine! There will be no television at all tonight for either of you!

VIOLA
She's treating us like children again.

BERTY
Don't I hear it.
(Tosses yet another pill)
There, I think that just about does it. I got three left. How many you taking?

VIOLA
One. This is for my heart.

BERTY
This one's for my blood pressure, my heart, and this one just gives me a nice buzz.

VIOLA
And don't you be charging us for those we didn't take, neither.

BERTY
Cheers! Now this doesn't mean we're friends.

VIOLA
Not at all.

BERTY
Fine. Bottoms up, then!

VIOLA
Cheers!

ROBIN
Ugh!

LIGHTS

Scene 3

(The walls are decorated with Christmas decorations. ROBIN, enters s.r. pushing in BERTY. She is dressed in her Sunday best, including her handbag.)

ROBIN
It's a real shame, it being Christmas and all. Only a few residents haven't come down with the flu: you, Miss Viola, and Lyle.

BERTY
Well, don't you go setting me by that ole pervert, Lyle, again. That man can't keep his dirty ole hands to himself. (aside) Maybe I wouldn't mind so much --- But he stinks. Don't y'all ever bathe that man?

ROBIN
We bathe him. Same as we bathe you. He just has accidents is all.

BERTY
Well, you gonna have an accident if you sets me next to him. Hear?

ROBIN
Yes, ma'am. Where do you want me to set you?

BERTY
Oh, anywhere's fine.

ROBIN
(pushing towards window)
How about here?

BERTY
No! No! For heaven's sakes it's too drafty!

ROBIN
(pushing off stage left)
Here's a nice warm spot.

BERTY
Fool! How am I gonna see what's going on?!

ROBIN
Ain't nobody here yet!

BERTY
Okay, okay dear. I'm not difficult. Just leave me anywhere. I don't mind. I'm just sitting around marking time, anyway. Whether it be by draft or boredom, it makes no difference, death is on my front porch. I can hear him knocking on the screen door now. *(Hollering)* "Be right there, just saying my good-byes!" So, anywhere dear. Here is just fine. Don't worry about me. Stick me in a closet. It's just a matter of time, anyway.

ROBIN
Why don't we just set you over here. By the magazines. Look, here's a People.

BERTY
Is it a new one, 'cause I read all the old ones. I don't want any old news. Is it new? If it isn't new, then I don't want it.

ROBIN
            (shoving it in her lap and rushing off s.r.)
It's fresh off the presses, Miss Berty!

BERTY
1978! How I do love keeping up to date.

(VIOLA is wheeled in by ROBIN. Again VIOLA is dressed in her Sunday best, again she carries her handbag, and wears her shawl.)

VIOLA
My, my, my I am a bit parched, honey. A little eggnog would be ever so nice about now. And don't forget the rum, either. Thank you, honey.

ROBIN
Here we go, Miss VIOLA, you'll have a nice view from the window over here.

VIOLA
Pardon me, but the last time you left me by the window it
rained and I got drenched. I'm lucky I didn't get pneumonia
and die. Or was that the plan?

ROBIN
(rolling her over s.l.)
How about over by the heater, then? You'll be nice and toasty.

VIOLA
By the steam heater? With my arthritis? Why don't you just
take a sledgehammer to my kneecaps? Now, honey don't you
think I'm too old to know what you're trying to do. This is
neglect, indisputable, unmistakable negligence, and I will
inform my son of this. Don't think for a second that I won't.
My Rudolph is an attorney in Baton Rouge. He will sue this
institution for every cent it has. Which judging from the food
and service, wouldn't be much. Never the less, watch your
step. I've got my eye on all of you.

ROBIN
Where would you like to sit, then, Miss VIOLA?

VIOLA
Oh, anywhere, for goodness sakes! What do I care. Just don't
put me next to that Lyle person.

ROBIN
Well, there's Miss Berty! You remember Miss Berty. She's
your old pill tossing buddy. You two have a lot in common.

VIOLA
(loud whisper)
I don't think so.

BERTY
Doubt it.

ROBIN
(wheels VIOLA over to opposite side of mag. table)
Yes! You all can discuss the different ways you can drive me
crazy. There you go. Now, you all have a nice chat before
your children come.
(exits)

VIOLA
(ringing bell)
Oh, Robin! I forgot something in my room!

ROBIN *(o.s.)*
Be right back!

BERTY
Don't forget to turn the heat up.

(The two women look at each other, give a quick smile, then look away.)

VIOLA
I hope you don't mind, Miss--Betty?

BERTY
Berty.

VIOLA
What's that, dear?

BERTY
The name's Berty.

VIOLA
Of course, that's what I said, Miss Berty. But I have a bit of a
sore throat. Must be getting that flu, after all. I don't feel
much like talking today. You understand.

BERTY
Suits me fine. Violet.

VIOLA
Viola.

BERTY
What? You say something?

VIOLA
Nothing.
(picking a magazine randomly)
Just --- it's Viola.

BERTY
You speaking to me?

VIOLA
No. No. *(pause)* My name isn't Violet, I've always hated that name. It's Viola. Same as my grandmother.

BERTY
That's nice. Now if you'll excuse me, I 'm reading a very interesting article.

VIOLA
Of course.
(she flips through a magazine)

(BERTY becomes seemingly absorbed in her People, VIOLA picks up another magazine and starts flipping through it. Then she begins to ring her bell.)

VIOLA
(ringing)
Yoo Hoo, Robin!
(stops ringing)
I'm terribly sorry, but I would like my eggnog, now!
(resumes ringing)
Yoo Hoo!

BERTY
They won't come.

VIOLA
What?

BERTY
I said, they won't come.

VIOLA
But that's what we pay them for. They most certainly will come!
(resumes ringing)

(BERTY shrugs and struggles to return to her article. VIOLA continues to ring her bell for awhile. Finally, her arm tiring, she quits.)

VIOLA
I'll be sure and tell my Rudolph about this.

BERTY
It won't do any good.

VIOLA
My son is an attorney!

BERTY
So is mine.
(VIOLA laughs)

BERTY
Why is that funny?

VIOLA
It must be my hearing, dear, but I - (laughs) I thought you said your son was an attorney. *(laughs)*

BERTY
I did.
(she slaps the magazine down on the table)

VIOLA
Oh. Well how absolutely lovely. I have always said that in this country it doesn't matter where you come from. A person can pull himself right out of the gutter if he has a mind to.

BERTY
The gutter?

VIOLA
Just a figure of speech.

BERTY
I'll have you know that my Charles was top of his class. Won a scholarship to Princeton, then went on to Yale.

VIOLA
Why of course he did! I am so glad they give you colored folks scholarships. I mean how else are you ever going to be able to compete?

BERTY
Charles did not win a scholarship for his color.
VIOLA
Oh? Did he play football or basketball, then?

BERTY
Neither.

VIOLA
Oh! Baseball! I have always enjoyed the great American pastime of baseball! I can remember going to games with my Daddy... Umm, hotdogs, and fresh roasted peanuts, why I can smell those -

BERTY
Charles did not win a scholarship for sports! He won it for his intelligence. Which – he got from me. His was an academic award.

VIOLA
No need to get defensive, dear. I'm sure he's as intelligent as he can be, all things considered. And it's so nice to hear that that firm action is working for somebody!

BERTY
I believe it's called affirmative action.

VIOLA
Why, that's just what I said! You people have certainly come a long way.

BERTY
You haven't.

VIOLA
Beg your pardon?

BERTY
I say, you obviously haven't.

VIOLA
Oh?
(She reaches out and grabs the People and begins flipping through it.)

BERTY
Yes, "oh".

(BERTY reaches down to grab the People back up; it isn't there. She sorts through the others, then glances over at VIOLA who is holding it up in front of her face.)

BERTY
I was reading that.

Broads on the Boards

VIOLA
This?

BERTY
Yes.
(she stretches out her hand)

VIOLA
You put it down.

BERTY
But I wasn't finished.

VIOLA
But you put it down.

BERTY
But I wasn't finished.

VIOLA
I'm in the middle of a very interesting article. Just a moment,
please.

BERTY
' beg your pardon, but so was I.

VIOLA
What do you want with this? It's all about white people,
anyway.

BERTY
Seems everything is all about white people. We get use to it
after awhile. Now hand it over.

VIOLA
Don't you order me about, you, you ---Negress!

BERTY
Now I know you can do better than that, honey!

(BERTY grabs for the magazine, gets it, but knocks all the other magazines off the table and drops the People in the process.)

VIOLA
Well, I never!

BERTY
Well, now you have.

VIOLA
(rings her bell furiously)
Yoo Hoo!

BERTY
Orderly! Orderly!

(After a few beats go by...)

BERTY
Oh, it's no use, they won't come!

VIOLA
(quits ringing)
That's what we pay them for!

BERTY
We don't pay them. That's the problem. Our children pay them. They listen to our children. Not us.

VIOLA
But it's my money.

BERTY
It may be your money. But they sign the check every month, don't they?

VIOLA
But - but it's from my account! It's always been from my account. It's my nest egg.

BERTY
Yes, well maybe you haven't noticed, but you're no longer sitting on that egg. Better get use to it.

VIOLA
I will not. Just wait till my son arrives today. I will let him know what I think of this place. Before I came here I was at St. Augustine's in Le Fourche parish. It was lovely. You rang a bell and someone always came. It was a private nursing home.

BERTY
This is a private nursing home.

VIOLA
Yes I suppose for - some - it is. But St. Augustine's was, how shall I say it---

BERTY
Yes, how shall you say it?

VIOLA
It was---more private.

BERTY
You mean no colored.

VIOLA
No, I didn't say that. I just meant it was more exclusive.

BERTY
I see. Exclusive.

VIOLA
Yes. That's correct. Exclusive. I'm only here temporarily. Until Rudolph straightens out my finances.

BERTY
Oh, and did Rudolph tell you when that might be? Today, maybe.

VIOLA
A month, maybe six weeks. He says we bought when we should have sold, or something like that.

BERTY
I see, handles your investments, too then?

VIOLA
Of course. Doesn't your son?

BERTY
'fraid so. That's why I'm here. You see, I brought up Charles to be a smart boy. He learned well. There's no sense in throwing away good money on an investment that ain't ever going to bring in returns, see? So here I am at the Sun Set Inn. And here you are too. Lot cheaper than St. Augustine's, if you get my point? Not that we can blame them. Charles has a family of his own now. Got a boy and a girl. Spitting image of their Daddy, too.

VIOLA
I got two granddaughters. Look just like me when I was a girl. Rudolph, he's my only child, he married a Catholic, though. I told him it wouldn't work out. What with them going to confession and all. Why if you ask me, that gives a person an easy way out of sinning! Little theft here, little adultery there, and go on into one of them closets they got and--- swish! They wipe the slate clean. Bit too simple if you ask me. But Rudolph, he didn't want to hear about it, too impressed by her endowments, if you know what I mean? So, he went ahead and got married. And I tried to like her, why I like – everyone, you know. But these modern girls, they have such strange notions 'bout doing things! She was nursing them at three years old, can you imagine?

BERTY
Three-years old?!

VIOLA
Simply scandalous, I say! And then they spoiled them and wouldn't spank them, either.

BERTY
A good wallop on the bottom can put things in the proper perspective, I say.

VIOLA
"That's child abuse!" she tells me. "Rudolph," I say, "did I ever abuse you?" "Well, Mama," he says, and proceeds to tell me how I left him emotionally scarred, scarred he says, when I smacked his bottom for using the f-word in school.

BERTY
I wouldn't take it too seriously. It's easier to blame your Mama than it is to blame yourself.

VIOLA
I never did it.

BERTY
No, neither did I.

VIOLA
If you ask me, it's all these talk shows they have nowadays.

BERTY
Could be. Imagine going on Oprah and talking about how mean your mama was to you growing up? Why, my Mama was the greatest woman ever did live. Came out of slavery, raised seven children and made sure we all learned to read and write.

VIOLA
My Mama had ten.

BERTY

My goodness a busy woman!

VIOLA

Can you believe we were nine girls! But Papa wanted a boy.
To carry on the family name, he said. I was the third child, and
seems I can't ever remember a time when Mama wasn't big
with child.

BERTY

So, she finally gave him that son he wanted so badly, eh?

VIOLA

She did.   And she died. Funny, she had ten and died, and I
had one and the doctor said, better not have anymore. I can
tell you that I made sure there wouldn't be anymore.

BERTY

Well, I had Charles, then Suzette. Suzette's out in California.
She's doing something with computers. She told me what, but
I couldn't understand it really. But she makes a good bit of
money I guess. Not married. But I don't push. Marriage isn't
for everyone. Maybe not even for anyone. Certainly not for
women.

VIOLA

I do declare, you have a point there. My husband, Richard,
he's been dead almost ten years now.

BERTY

I'm sorry to hear that.

VIOLA

Are you? I'm not. Old goat expired in his mistress' arms. In
the hourly rate room at the Lion's Den Lodge . He didn't even
have the decency to take her to a Holiday Inn. His cronies
tried to cover for him. Said he had been at a business meeting
there. As if I would believe that a man in real estate would do
business at the Lion's Den Lodge in nothing but his –

VIOLA (CONT.)
--undershorts! What exactly was he trying to sell?

BERTY
That must have been a shock.

VIOLA
The death? Yes. The philandering? No. He'd been sneaking around for years. In some ways I didn't really mind. As long as he came to our bed exhausted, it was fine by me. Never did understand what all the fuss is about (whispers) S-E-X, anyway.

BERTY
I preferred canasta, myself. At least after my first husband. Now that man, um-umm, I never knew so much fun could be free. That was Simon. He was a good man. Never cheated, never drank, loved the Lord. But he died young.

VIOLA
Now, that is a tragedy.

BERTY
Seems I cried myself to sleep for a year. For a few years it was just me and the children. Then I met my second husband. Now when he died, I danced on his grave!

VIOLA
Oh my, why's that?

BERTY
That man had his own ideas about marriage, let me tell you. And they were nothing like anything I had ever experienced. "Do this, don't do that, stay home, don't have friends," and for awhile it was okay. I mean I was so terribly lonely after my first husband died I suppose I would have put up with anything. I did, too. When the kids were small I was so busy I didn't have time to do much else except care for them and him. But once they were grown, I wanted more ---

VIOLA
I know.

BERTY
I wanted to work, to---

VIOLA
To explore---

BERTY
To have fun---

VIOLA
To live!

BERTY
Uh-huh.

VIOLA
Uh-huh.

BERTY
But he didn't understand.

VIOLA
Did not.

BERTY
Wanted me to stay home. Waiting for him.
VIOLA
Dinner on the table.

BERTY
House all spanking clean.

VIOLA
And us looking fresh as daisies.

BERTY
"You're getting too fat!"

VIOLA
You're getting too thin!"

BERTY
And him coming home smelling of liquor.

VIOLA
Or perfume.

BERTY
Uh-huh.

VIOLA
Oh, yeah.

BERTY
He died about 15 years ago.

VIOLA
Please accept my condolences.

BERTY
If you'll accept mine.

(They nod at each other.)

VIOLA
I wonder what time it is? Rudolph said he was coming before lunchtime. When's yours coming?

BERTY
They like to surprise me.

VIOLA
That's so sweet! I can't wait to see my granddaughters. Their mama spoils them, but they are adorable, and smart as whips!

BERTY
Mine, too. You remember being that smart when you was little?

VIOLA
I don't think I ever been that smart! They started using computers in first grade!

BERTY
And reading before they got to kindygarten!

(VIOLA opens her locket to show BERTY her photos.)

VIOLA
Here are my darlings! That's Star and that's Moonbeam.

BERTY
You white people sure have some funny names!

VIOLA
It was that mother of theirs. Secretly I call them Sara and Mary Ann.

BERTY
Aren't they sweet! How old are they?

VIOLA
Here they're 5 and 7. I haven't gotten any new pictures in a while.

BERTY
How old are they now?

VIOLA
15 and 17.

BERTY
Oh. Well. I'm sure you'll get some new ones real soon. Let me show you mine.

(BERTY reaches into her purse and pulls out a couple of snapshots.)

BERTY
This here's Tessa. And this is Albert. Named after me.
Alberta's my given name. She's 8 and he'll be 6 on his next
birthday.

VIOLA
(taking the photos)
Oh, I just love how you folks can do that to your hair! When I
was a little girl, about 5, before I knew better you understand, I
use to play with this little Negro girl who had her hair done up
like this. Pieces of colorful ribbon tied in bows all over. Well
one day, I begged her to do my hair up just like hers. And she
did. I don't know what kind of job she did, 'cause she wasn't
much older than myself, I don't suppose it much mattered,
though. When I got home that evening, my daddy grabbed me
by my hair, and slapped me so hard I fell over. Told me I
looked like a pickaninny, that I ought to be ashamed of my
self. I went to my bedroom and my older sister tried to help
me take out the braids and the bits of ribbon. Some of it
wouldn't come undone and we had to cut it out, clear up to my
scalp. How I cried when I saw myself in the mirror. And all
that pretty ribbon lying in the trash. Oh, but I looked a fright!
I tell you!

BERTY
And the little girl? Did you still play with her?

VIOLA
Heavens no! Daddy would have surely tanned my hide if I did!
I suppose she found children her own color to play with.
That's how things were. My daddy taught me that.

BERTY
Birds of a feather flock together, don't you know.

VIOLA
That's what Daddy always said. But nowadays, why everything
is so confused.

BERTY
Just plain crazy!

VIOLA
If you ask me, things'd be a lot better if your people would stay
with your people and mine would stay with mine. But all this
integration, well no wonder there's so much hatred in the
world!

BERTY
Well, of course! What with you folks always trying to keep us
down!

VIOLA
It's not that we keep you down, it's that you all are so jealous
of us! You want what we got. But that can't be, surely you
agree?

BERTY
Say again. Why can't that be?

VIOLA
Well, that's obvious.
(VIOLA holds out her hand)
What do you see there?

BERTY
A wrinkled old hand.

VIOLA
A wrinkled---! Well, yes it may be a little wrinkled, and it surely
isn't young, but it is also white. That there is a wrinkled, old,
white hand. And that is a wrinkled, old, black hand. See?

BERTY
Oh, I see. What I don't see is what that has to do with anything.

VIOLA
Right there! That is exactly what I mean! We open the doors to you people, desegregate the schools, the nursing homes even, and what do you folks do in return? You get uppity, that's what you do. You all forget your place!

BERTY
Well, remind me then, Miss Violet, just what is my place?

VIOLA
You are a Negro, Miss Berty!

BERTY
(looking at her hands)
I do believe you're right! Thank you, Lord!

VIOLA
Fine, jest if you will. But the fact remains, as a white woman I am your superior. Like it or not.

BERTY
If you're so superior, why you sitting in a wheelchair, in a nursing home, waiting for the Good Lord to call your number, same as me?

VIOLA
Same as you?! I am not the same as you.

BERTY
No, you're a heck of a lot uglier!

VIOLA
How dare you give me such lip! The Bible says that the Lord God made man in his image. It does not say anything 'bout him being colored.

BERTY
Doesn't say anything 'bout him being a woman neither. So just
how do you figure into that plan, Miss Violet?

VIOLA
(glares at BERTY, then rings her bell)
Orderly! Orderly!

BERTY
Robin, come get this woman! She's foulin' the air with her
white superiority!

VIOLA
Orderly!

BERTY
Hurry, the stench is suffocating me!

LIGHTS

Scene 4

(*The walls are now hung with posters of Dr. Martin Luther King, Jr.
There are even some streamers and a few balloons. BERTY, all dressed
up is watching a t.v. program. VIOLA is wheeled in by ROBIN.*)

VIOLA
They should be here about 1 o'clock. What time do you have,
honey?

ROBIN
Five minutes later than last time you asked.

VIOLA
Am I repeating myself? (laughs) It's just that I'm so excited.
And---

(looking around at the walls)
---look how pretty you decorated! Who told you it was my birthday? Was it my son? Why that little stinker, I told him not to make a fuss.

ROBIN
But, Miss Viola---

VIOLA
How old do you suppose I am?

ROBIN
Sweet 16?

VIOLA
No, silly. Really. How old do I look?

ROBIN
I'd say about 65.

VIOLA
Really? Well, I am 75 years old today.

ROBIN
That's remarkable. You don't look a day over 65.

VIOLA
I always did take good care of myself. Oh, how I do love balloons! Fetch me one of them and I'll tie it right here on the arm of my chair.

ROBIN
Sure, Happy Birthday. *(exits)*

VIOLA
Why, it looks just like its dancing! (sings) "Dancing in the dark---"

BERTY
Shhh!

VIOLA *(pause)*
"If I like a you, and you like a me, and we like a both---"

BERTY
Hush, can't you see I'm watching Jimmy Swaggert?

VIOLA
I'm so sorry. Pardon me.
(pause then singing softly)
"Tea for two, and two for tea, that's you for me and me for---"

BERTY
Do- you- mind?

VIOLA
Why of course not. Please, don't let me disturb you. Let it never be known that Viola Thibidoux kept someone from having her soul saved. *(pause)* Even if today is my birthday.

BERTY
Happy Birthday. Now, hush up.
VIOLA
I'm 75-years old. It's a mile-stone.

BERTY
Well la-dee-dah. 80 is the big one.

VIOLA
You're 80!

BERTY
Almost. Shhh!

VIOLA
Why I would have never guessed. 'Course you folks never look your age. Wish I had skin like you.

BERTY
You wish you was colored?

VIOLA
Oh, heavens no! (Laughs) I just wish we white folks had whatever it is you all have in your skin. You know, to keep it so young looking.

BERTY
I see.

VIOLA
It's so sweet how they all decorated this place for my birthday. *(looks around)* But, why do you suppose that colored man's picture's everywhere?

BERTY
What?

VIOLA
I say, who is that colored man all over the walls?

BERTY
Don't you know what day it is today?

VIOLA
Of course, it's my birthday! I'm 75 years old.

BERTY
Fine, it's your birthday and your 75. But what else is today?

VIOLA
Why, I believe it's Monday. And Rudolph and the children are coming to see me. They sure are.

BERTY
Alright. How do you suppose they all can get away from work and school on a Monday?

VIOLA
That's simple. It's my birthday!

BERTY
It is also a national holiday.

VIOLA
My birthday is a national holiday!

BERTY
No your birthday isn't, (*pointing*) his is!

VIOLA
Well, who the heck is he?!

BERTY
Oh, for Pete's sake, that's Dr. Martin Luther King. Don't tell me you don't remember him?

VIOLA
Of course I heard of him! I'm Protestant ain't I? He's that fellow who pounded the 96 thesis onto the church door! But I didn't know he was colored. How do you like that?

BERTY
(*pointing*) Martin Luther King, *Jr.*, honey.

VIOLA
The Protestant's son?

BERTY
No! The man you're talking about died several centuries ago. Dr. King was assassinated in 1963. You <u>must</u> remember. He was a great civil rights leader. He lead marches on Washington, bus boycotts in Alabama. You remember Rosa Parks?

VIOLA
I don't believe I've met her. What parish is she from? Don't you roll your eyes at me. I'm 75 years old! How am I suppose to remember every colored person in history? I remember important people. Like George Washington, and Thomas Jefferson, and --- and Lincoln. Hey there, he freed you all, didn't he! But you can't expect me to remember everybody that ever did any little thing. I am, after all, 75-years old!

BERTY
Dr. King didn't do a little thing!

VIOLA
Oh, yeah? Then why don't I remember him?

BERTY
Maybe because you're senile.

VIOLA
I am not senile!

BERTY
You are 75-years old!

VIOLA
So you're 80!

BERTY
But I got good skin.

ROBIN
(enters bearing a piece of cake with a candle burning in it)
Miss Viola, your son just called. Seems a business emergency came up and he's not going to make it. I'm sorry.

VIOLA
But I'm 75-years old today! Well, is she coming? She could at least bring the grandchildren.

ROBIN
I don't believe so, ma'am. I'm sure they'll make it up to you next year.

VIOLA
There may not be a next year!

BERTY
She's 75-years old!

VIOLA
How could they miss my birthday? At Easter it was they were going to Hawaii, Mother's Day they went to Palm Beach, Fourth of July he was sick, okay fine, I understood, but this is my birthday!

BERTY
My children are the same way. No use crying about it. Do like I do. Live a long time and cost them plenty.

ROBIN
Listen here, we still have the cake. And the balloons.

VIOLA
Those---
          (untying the balloon and letting it go)
---are Dr. King's balloons.

BERTY
I don't think he'd mind if you had one.

VIOLA
Well, I don't know...I never took anything from a colored man before.

ROBIN
We won't tell. Now what do you say you blow out that candle before there's wax all over your cake?

BERTY
Go on, I know you got a lotta wind in you.

(Viola smiles, blows out the candle).

BERTY & ROBIN
Happy Birthday to you!
        (they clap)

VIOLA
Thank you, that was so sweet.

ROBIN
(hands VIOLA the piece of cake)
Enjoy, Miss Viola *(exits)*

BERTY
Hey, where's my piece?

ROBIN (o.s.)
You know you're not suppose to have sugar!

VIOLA
Umm...I have always loved chocolate cake.

BERTY
That's a mighty big piece. I could see how you might not want
to finish the whole thing.

VIOLA
So, tell remind me about this Dr. King. He's starting to look
familiar.

BERTY
Well of course he is! (pause) Tell you what: You give me some
of that cake and I'll tell you.

VIOLA
But you're not supposed to.

BERTY
I'm supposed to have peace in my old age and I got you, don't
I? Give me some of that cake.

VIOLA
I'll save you some.

BERTY
Some frosting, too.
    (VIOLA nods)
Dr. King believed in social change through peaceful
demonstration.

VIOLA
You mean kinda like --- Jesus?

BERTY
That's right. Like Jesus. You're eating all the frosting!
VIOLA
And you say someone killed him?

BERTY
How can you not remember? Yes. Yes, a white man shot him
dead.

VIOLA
Dr. King married?

BERTY
Yes'm. And children. Whites tried to kill them too. But
Reverend King was the one they were really after. And they
got him.

VIOLA
He was a man of the cloth?

BERTY
Yes, ma'am. A man of God.

VIOLA
My, my, my...why they want a go and do a fool thing like that for? Folks go to hell for adultery, my Richard did, imagine what you'd get for killing a preacher?

BERTY
Seems some folks thought he was being too uppity. Now hand over that cake.

VIOLA
(she does)
Sort of like you. But I wouldn't go and kill you.

BERTY
(wipes off fork, looks it over real good)
Glad to hear it. Umm that's good. But then again I'm not challenging your whole way of life.

VIOLA
Like Hades you ain't! I had some interesting birthdays before, but can't ever remember one that I shared my birthday cake with a colored woman.

BERTY
Can't say I ever shared one with a white woman before. Happy birthday, Viola.

VIOLA
Thank you, Berty.
(gets the balloon dancing again)
"It had to be you...

BERTY
"...not somebody new..."

LIGHTS

Scene 5

(The walls are now decorated for Thanksgiving. BERTY is dressed in her best dress. VIOLA is simply in a flannel nightgown and her shawl. VIOLA seems to be frailer, and not as spunky. ROBIN wheels in BERTY and starts to exit.)

VIOLA
I been sitting here for quite some time now, and I really have to---

ROBIN
We're real short staffed today, Miss Viola, I'll be right back.
(exits)

VIOLA
I'll be here. So, did you have a nice Thanksgiving with your family?

BERTY
Well, they got here this time, at least. Yours?

VIOLA
No. *(pause, then softly . . .)*
Was I really such an awful mother?

BERTY
Well . . . of course you weren't! You're not crying are you?

VIOLA
No. Yes. I mean, why doesn't he want to visit me? Wasn't I a good mother?

BERTY
Oh, now, you know . . . they all got busy lives.

VIOLA
It's Thanksgiving!

BERTY

I know, I know but when they're married and they got in-laws .
. they'll come next year, I'm sure.

VIOLA

That's what Rudolph said: they had to go to Her family's in
Mississippi this year. Next year they are going to come and get
me. Oh, Berty, it will be lovely. I gave her all my china and
silver when I entered St. Augustine's. The table will be set with
real linen, and candles. We have a candelabra that has been
passed down in our family since the days of General Lee. I
always set a beautiful table.

BERTY

Me, too. Everybody had a job in our family. Charles put out
the plates and the glasses. Suzette set out the silver and
napkins. When Simon was still alive he'd fix his famous sweet
potatoes. Umm they were delicious. Now my second
husband, he just sat on his fat ass in front of the television.
BERTY (CONT.)
Yellin' in every fifteen minutes: "Is it supper, yet?" That part
of Thanksgiving I don't miss. My, it is cold in here.

VIOLA

Wasn't that turkey horrible, today?

BERTY

Oo, was it ever dried out!

VIOLA

And those potatoes --- they using a mix, I am certain.

BERTY

Why, I am sure! Did you get any gravy?

VIOLA
Uh-huh, you?

BERTY
No. They keep trying to get me to lose a few pounds. For what, I say? I tell 'em, I ain't dating no more. For Pete's sake I am 80 years old. Least they could do is give me a little gravy on my dry turkey.

VIOLA
You didn't miss much. It was real watery. Matter of fact if they don't dry it out, they think they gotta make everything into mush. I may not have my teeth, but they don't have to serve me baby food.

BERTY
I hear you! Cream corn, cream spinach, cream broccoli, they'd give us cream bread if they could.

VIOLA
The bread is in the oven.

BERTY
What?

VIOLA
Mama, the bread is almost ready. I can crumble it up for you. Jasmine did it last time, Mama. Please, let me.

BERTY
            (awkward pause)
Dang, it is cold in here! Robin, Robin, turn up that thermostat!

VIOLA
The year after Mama died, me and my sisters wanted to have Thanksgiving as usual. We were all pretty young. Gladys, my oldest sister, she been dead almost 20 years now, she was only 'bout 12 at the time. Years past we had always helped Mama, but helping isn't the same as overseeing the whole thing. My, that kitchen was a sight for sore eyes!

BERTY
I can just imagine! Nine girls you were?

VIOLA
Uh-huh, the youngest being two. How they kept getting under our feet!

BERTY
Gotta have somebody in charge of the little ones.

VIOLA
Of course, but wasn't nobody in charge of us big ones! So we did the best we could. And dinner was a little later than usual, put when we called Daddy to the table it was set, even had the candelabra lit, been in the family since the revolutionary war.

BERTY
Thought you said since General Lee?

VIOLA
Did I? Well, anyhow it was old, and it was lit, and things looked a lot like the year before when Mama was still with us. Daddy sat at the head of the table and he looked so proud. Told us so. Then he started carving the turkey. We filled up his dish with all the trimmings. Said Grace, and then we waited for Daddy to take his first bite. He took a fork full of potatoes, and tasted them and nodded. Then he took a fork of the yams, and nodded. Then he sliced off a bit of the turkey, he started to nod, but then this little crease appeared between his eyes, he chewed, then he scrunched up his face and spit that turkey right out on the table.

BERTY
What was wrong with it? Too dry? Too salty?

VIOLA
Too soapy.

BERTY
What?

VIOLA
Seems when Gladys told Bernice to wash out the turkey good, she had. With lye soap.

BERTY
Oh, no!

VIOLA
Oh, yes! The turkey was permeated with a taste of soapsuds. It's funny now, but Daddy didn't find it funny in the least. He picked that turkey up by its remaining leg, went to the front door, brought his arm way back and threw that bird as far as he could.

BERTY
And then what happened?

VIOLA
Oh, well it landed in the big oak by the mailbox, and there it perched till spring. My, my, my what must the other birds have thought?

BERTY
No, what happened with your daddy?

VIOLA
Oh, he kept going. Didn't come back until after midnight. Never said a word to any of us.

BERTY
Guess it was just one more reminder that your Mama was gone and things were never going to be the same. Course, he should have thought of that when he was dreaming of a son after the woman gave him nine daughters. Robin! Robin! What are you trying to freeze an old lady?!

VIOLA
Oh, my! (she starts ringing her bell)

BERTY
Isn't it cold in here?

VIOLA
No, I've got to go.
      (rings furiously)

BERTY
You don't have any place to go, what you talking about?

VIOLA
No, I have got to go. *(ringing)* Oh, where is that girl?

BERTY
They are real short today, on account of the holiday.
Just hold on for a minute.

VIOLA
I can't much longer.

BERTY
Robin! Somebody get in here right now!

VIOLA
Oh, Berty!

BERTY *(grabs the bell)*
I cannot believe these people! Can't they let us keep our
dignity?

VIOLA
I been sitting in here for hours.

BERTY
Why you been sitting in here by yourself? Why don't you just
stay in your room? Robin!!

VIOLA
I - I wanted to see you.

BERTY
Me?

VIOLA
Yes. I, oh, it's too horrible to say.

BERTY
I know. You were hoping my family hadn't shown up, weren't you?

(VIOLA nods)
BERTY
Well, they showed, and they fed me in my bed, like some old invalid. They fed me that tasteless, mushy, thanksgiving dinner. And I let them. The children looked bored, and Charles' wife just looked uncomfortable. Charles? Well, he –
BERTY (CONT.)
-- had that look in his eye, you know the one.

VIOLA
Pity.

BERTY
Uh-huh. He has this pinched look on his face. As if the stench of death were clinging to me. I ask him what he's been up to and right away he looks guilty. And she jumps in and says he's been very busy with his law practice. I'm not accusing him of anything, I say. Just inquiring 'bout his life, is all. I have a right to know about his life, don't I? "Don't shout, Mama," he says, "You're frightening the children". I glance over at them, and sure enough, they look terrified. So, now not only have I made my son pity me, and feel guilty, I have frightened my grandchildren. You can be sure I was very thankful for their visit. Does that make you feel better?

VIOLA
Of course, not.
(she resumes ringing the bell hard)
Maybe a little.

BERTY
Good, I'm glad someone got some pleasure from my son's visit. So, did you have a horrible day, too?

VIOLA
Absolutely horrible. Is that what you came in here to find out?
(rings)

BERTY
Yes, Miss Viola, I am ashamed to say it is.

VIOLA
Oh, dear . . .

(She looks down at her lap, she pulls her blanket up over her face.)
BERTY
Damn, these people! Damn, old age! Robin, get your butt in here this instant!

(VIOLA is still staring straight ahead.)

BERTY
Now don't you fret. This sort of thing happens to everybody. Why I remember when---

VIOLA
Oh, my goodness! *(giggles)* Can I touch your hair?

BERTY
Say, what?

VIOLA
Ooo, I just love those pretty ribbons.

BERTY
What---?

VIOLA
Do mine, Mary Ann! Please!

BERTY
You want me to braid your hair?

VIOLA
Uh-huh, just like you. Please!

BERTY
No, I don't think that's ---

VIOLA
Pretty Please!!!

BERTY
Lord, I must be going senile---
(BERTY pulls a ribbon out of her own hair and begins to braid VIOLA's.)

BERTY (CONT.)
When your son sees this they gonna throw my wrinkled old butt out of here. They sure are. Uh-huh.

VIOLA
Sing.

BERTY
What?!

VIOLA
Sing me that song, you know the one ...la, la, la-la...
("Go Tell It on the Mountain")

BERTY
Huh?

VIOLA
La, la, la-la...

BERTY
You don't mean.... "Go Tell It on the Mountain"?

VIOLA
Yes! That's my favorite! Sing, it, please!

BERTY
    (does a quick look about)
"Go tell it on the mountain, over the hill and —"

VIOLA & BERTY
"—everywhere! Go tell it on the mountain—"

LIGHTS

Scene 6

(Later the same day. VIOLA alone on stage, slumped in her chair. ROBIN enters.)

ROBIN
Time for bed, Miss Viola.

(ROBIN shakes VIOLA's shoulder.)

ROBIN
Miss Viola? Miss Viola!

(She reaches for VIOLA's wrist to take her pulse.)

ROBIN
Oh, no! Just hang in there, honey, just hang on!

LIGHTS

Scene 7

(The walls are hung with Valentine decorations. Late evening. VIOLA is again in her nightgown. She has had a stroke, and her right side is paralyzed. BERTY is sitting with her knitting in her lap.)

BERTY
It won't be so bad. I hear them nurses over at that place are real good. Why I bet you ring a bell over there and someone will come right away! Yes, bet they'll take real good care of you. *(pause)* The food can't be any worse. (pause) And you sure won't be putting up with this ole' uppity colored woman! I hear the place you going to is, how did you say? Real exclusive. Seems like your son is breaking open the piggy bank this time. Doctor must have told 'em your days are numbered. Oh, now why did you say that, Bertie! Now, you just go on and do what I told you, hear? You hang on there a good long while and make 'em pay. –
BERTY (CONT.)
Why sure, you keep ringing that bell, honey! You keep ringing it hard!

ROBIN
(enters with VIOLA's coat and handbag)
It's time to go now, Miss Viola. Okay, Miss Berty?

BERTY
She's ready. We said our good byes.

ROBIN
Aw, now. It ain't good bye! You'll see each other again!

BERTY
Why do you all insist on treating us like imbeciles?

ROBIN
Why I never –

BERTY
You do. All the time. I know you mean well, but we're old, and we know a mite more about life than you do. I'd wish you'd all remember that.

ROBIN
I'm sorry, I never meant to –

BERTY
I know, hon. And me and her said good bye. Amazing we ever did get to say hello.

ROBIN
(begins pushing VIOLA out)
Okay...now don't you go sneaking any candy tonight.

BERTY
Who, me? And turn the heat up in here before you leave. You trying to freeze an old lady?
VIOLA
(tries to speak)
Burie...

(She pulls her shawl off awkwardly with her left hand. She reaches out with it to BERTY.)

BERTY
Oh, no, I couldn't...
(VIOLA tosses it on her lap.)

VIOLA
Take...
(BERTY does. She puts it around her shoulders.)

BERTY
Thank you.

(VIOLA nods)
(ROBIN wheels VIOLA out.)

BERTY
Hey, Violet, don't forget....
(gestures ringing the bell)
(VIOLA nods and rings the bell as she goes off stage).

THE END.

Production History

"Bra-vo" premiered at the Univ. of ND's Int'l Center, performed by Kathy Coudle-King

Compañeras was given a reading at the Association of Theatre and Higher Education Conference, Denver, and subsequently directed by Sarah Thames at the Hotchkiss School (CT) and Becky Becker at Colmbus State Univ. (GA), 2011

"Cookies" premiered at WomanSong, 2009, performed by Brianna Thompson

"Couple of Boobs" was first read in Chicago as part of a publishing party for *Conclave, a journal*, then performed at the Univ. of ND with Jill Vaagene and Joy Vaagene

"Drippings" was first performed by Betty Gard at the Empire Arts Center in GF, ND for a Hurricane Katrina fundraiser in 2006

Flesh & Bones (a.k.a. The Fat Lady Sings) was first performed at the Charlotte Danstrom Conference at the University of ND in 1992, with Sharyl Simeone originating the role of Billi & Christine Delea as Liz,

"Go Away" was first performed by Natasha Yearwood Thomas, directed by John Thompson in March 2005

"The Hole Story" was first directed by Adonica Schultz-Aune, performed by Donna Stewart and Cherie Johnson at the MN Shorts Festival, in Mankato, 2010

Milk Dreams was first performed at the Empire Arts Center, under the direction of Adonica Schultz-Aune, featuring the late Theresa Thompson Dafforn in 2002

"Mourning Coffee" was performed by Ohio State University as part of its Senior Theatre programming under the direction of Alan Woods

"No Room at the Cemetery" is part of *Off the Map*, *which* premiered in Buffalo, ND, role of Anne originated by Kathy Coudle-King, 2012

"Plantanos," first performed at Womansong, in LaMoure, ND in 2009 by Kathy Coudle-King

"Pulling Out All the Stops" was first performed by Cynthia Prom at the Fire Hall Theatre, New Year's Eve, 2009

Production History Continued

Ralph's Ark, commissioned by UND Center for Rural Health, 1995. Role of "Marge" originated by Janie Franz
"Scary Tales," premiered at WomanSong, 2009, performed by Kelly King
Las Soldaderas was commissioned by the Univ. of ND's Women Center, 2015. Audra Hendrickson, Isabel Rhen, Emily Walsh, and Kathy Coudle-King originated the roles
"Someone Borrowed, Someone Blue" was first produced by NJ Repertory in 2008
St. Bette's was first performed at Stella Adler at NYU as part of a senior showcase directed by Devanand Janki, 2010
Trees was first produced at the Dayton FutureFest in 2008
Women with Wrinkles was first performed by Toni Scott, Vicki Hampton-Mitzel, and Kay Mendick at the University of North Dakota in February, 1991

Copies of the full-length plays excerpted here can be purchased at www.dakotalit.com .

Forthcoming: **Her-story Alive: a collection of plays based on the lives of women in American history**. This collection will be published in 2016 and features "TRIANGLE," a one-act play about the rise of women labor activists preceding, during, and immediately following the Triangle Waistcoat Factory Fire, as told by Charlotte Perkins Gilman; Last Call, a full-length play based on a murder case involving Temperance activists at the end of the 19th century in Dakota Territory; and "Judith & Janey," a ten-minute play about a fictional encounter between Sakakawea and Julia Clark after Lewis and Clark return from their Voyage of Discovery.
Also, in 2016, look for **Listen to This: Plays about sexual abuse & violence against women.** Plays explore topics about stalking, domestic abuse, and date rape. These plays are perfect for educational settings and provide a great jumping off point for group discussion.

www.ingramcontent.com/pod-product-compliance
Lightning Source LLC
LaVergne TN
LVHW051232080426
835513LV00016B/1543